WISDOM of GABRIEL

Channelled messages from Arch Angel Gabriel

LISA HODGSON

BALBOA.
PRESS
A DIVISION OF HAY HOUSE

Copyright © 2014 Lisa Hodgson.

All rights reserved. No part of this book may be used or reproduced by any means, graphic, electronic, or mechanical, including photocopying, recording, taping or by any information storage retrieval system without the written permission of the publisher except in the case of brief quotations embodied in critical articles and reviews.

Balboa Press books may be ordered through booksellers or by contacting:

Balboa Press
A Division of Hay House
1663 Liberty Drive
Bloomington, IN 47403
www.balboapress.com.au
1 (877) 407-4847

Because of the dynamic nature of the Internet, any web addresses or links contained in this book may have changed since publication and may no longer be valid. The views expressed in this work are solely those of the author and do not necessarily reflect the views of the publisher, and the publisher hereby disclaims any responsibility for them.

The author of this book does not dispense medical advice or prescribe the use of any technique as a form of treatment for physical, emotional, or medical problems without the advice of a physician, either directly or indirectly. The intent of the author is only to offer information of a general nature to help you in your quest for emotional and spiritual well-being. In the event you use any of the information in this book for yourself, which is your constitutional right, the author and the publisher assume no responsibility for your actions.

Any people depicted in stock imagery provided by Thinkstock are models, and such images are being used for illustrative purposes only.
Certain stock imagery © Thinkstock.

Printed in the United States of America.

ISBN: 978-1-4525-2671-3 (sc)
ISBN: 978-1-4525-2672-0 (e)

Balboa Press rev. date: 11/14/2014

Contents

Wisdom of Love – Words from Gabriel 1
Wisdom of Children – Words from Gabriel 73
Wisdom of Time – Words from Gabriel 119

Foreword

"I was referred to Lisa about 4 years ago at a time in my life when I needed help" The accuracy in the messages I was given, was not only a testament to her amazing abilities and connection with the spirit world, but what truly makes her so good is her compassion towards people, there is a genuine care and love felt when you speak with Lisa. There's a reason she was able to channel these books, and that's because she has a heart of gold.

Tammy Lawson
Business owner and client

Preface

This book came about because I worked as a psychic and one day I had the urge to get my laptop out and just write down words that I was picking up. I never dreamt that I would be an author. I found that I was to channel words from ArchAngel Gabriel who is known as the Angel of communication as he came to Mary to announce her pregnancy with Jesus. Don't get me wrong I do not have tickets on myself and I never saw myself as a channeller. I am though, and I have since held channelling nights at my home for friends. Gabriel was not the first Angel I associated with and it was ArchAngel Michael whom I felt around me more. I suppose through this journey I have discovered that I can connect with any of them. What a blessing. My journey started with my son picking up things spiritual and I researched then lo and behold I found myself being told to read for a well-known reader who insisted I read for them. I bought a tarot deck to learn from and ended up reading in a little local new age shop. I developed a following and then eventually ended up being self employed as a psychic contractor on the largest psychic line in the southern hemisphere. I now work on another line and have a loyal following. I know I am gifted and I see it as a gift. I do not advertise it and am humble. This book is something I was instructed to do by spirit and I am again humbled they chose me. It may not be an erudite tome but it's my little contribution. This book is not meant to be accurate or gospel. It is merely a take on things according to ArchAngel Gabriel using my point of reference and me as a conduit. Hopefully it will touch the hearts of those that need it. Please enjoy this book and its three components which were the original three books now turned into one. I have more books coming so watch this space.

Blessings
Lisa

Acknowledgements

I acknowledge my parents and my brothers who even though we are on different wavelengths we are still family.

My thanks to my friends Jill, Tammy, Daniel, Doriana, Dawn, Kevin, Tennelle, Vickie and Lynchie for your support, love and friendship. Oh we have laughed and laughed and cried. All of you are so special to me and I am grateful I have you in my life for you guys have been there for me through everything. And thankyou to Annie for if it weren't for you I'd never have revisited my book.

I thank my teachers in life and mentors. I acknowledge my loved ones in spirit who I still have around me. I thank all my clients many of whom have become fast friends.

I want to thank Balboa for being so good to me.

I want to thank my beautiful Angels and I thankyou for being the reason I am doing what I am doing.

Lastly I want to thank my beautiful son Robert. You are the air that I breathe and the reason I am here. I was born to be the mother who raised a fine human being. You are everything to me. I dedicate this book to you, my son. You are the true gift.

Lisa

Wisdom of Love – Words from Gabriel

Introduction

It's just after ten in the evening on a Saturday and I have completed several tasks. I have done some artwork (I am an artist), crocheted a little (a hat for my mother in law), practised a dance routine (I also belly-dance). And just as I am about to turn in for the night with a good book and texting a conversation with a girlfriend I became aware that I was being poked in the ribs by my angels (who are yours too by the way) to get on with the project they had so kindly informed me I was to do. I was reluctant due to my pesky cat leaving his mark on my laptop case. I'd smothered it with disinfectant and was leaving it to dry. Lovely! Humph! But I got past my discomfort and here I am. A week ago these lovely Angels popped in to see me and guided me to write a short list of topics to discuss with you. It was announced (with a little fanfare) that I was to channel this book about Angels and their effect and presence in yours and my life. You see I am a psychic and a medium. I have recently been getting impulses to write about the topic I am familiar with. Angels. I am by no means an expert on these magnificent (and modest) beings but I have a lot of help from them on a daily basis. I diligently wrote down several topics for them and put the pad down with intent to look at it when time is right. So obviously the time is right, right now.

This is strange for me as I don't see myself as a writer let alone someone who channels. I was told years ago that I was a channel and that Francis of Assisi was someone whom I was to channel. I fobbed this off as I still didn't think it was possible. Being a medium as you can guess means I do channel. However I refuse to let anything take over me so I sort of semi-channel. I see dead people, sense spirit guides, feel and sometimes see Angels. You can imagine my surprise when They announced I was to 'channel' a book for them. Obviously I'm not the only one to have written a book on Angels and trust me I put that to them thinking 'Why me?'. But obviously they are very persuasive and they must have some faith in me.

I will try not to be preachy or (pardon pun) holier than thou. Like I said I'm not an expert but hope that my sense of humour and perception can give you some insight into the world of communicating with Angels. They want you to listen carefully and let your mind be free of any preconceptions. Be prepared to really try to hear their soft voices and feel their presences. Breathe them and love them. What a glorious support they have been for me and many others.

I am a single mum of a twelve year old boy who is also psychic and that is how I came to develop too. I read books on every topic regarding the psychic arts and children who are sensitive in order to be able to understand what my little fellow was experiencing. Eventually I was in a reading with another psychic who plonked her deck of tarot cards in front of me and told me to read for her as it was what I was supposed to do. The reading went better than I expected and I left wondering what this meant. I went to yet another psychic and was instantly attracted to the tarot deck she used. I immediately went to the nearest new age store (ironically the very one I would end up work in up until this day nine years later) and ordered a deck for myself. I practised on myself and friends and eventually plucked up the courage to advertise. At the time I only read the tarot as per the book. Gradually I would develop more skills such as sensing auras and feelings (you would know this as clairvoyance and clairsentience).

I had been psychic all my life but did not use it as at the time I was oblivious to it.

Now it was time to help people and I felt absolutely positive I could put a grin on someone's face and ease those who needed guidance.

I do have the tendency to throw myself in the deep end and ended up asking Veronica at a little shop in town if she had any vacancies for readers. She did as at the time there was only one reader there already. However she said that it was usually quite quiet. That didn't matter to me as I just needed the experience and believe it or not it was the best move as far as finding my abilities. Being in the hot seat, so to speak, made me fly by the seat of me pants. It opened up a whole new world to me that eventually would define the real me. I felt really at home and at ease doing readings for people and allowed spirit to push me to my limits with the experiences that came with the job. Gradually I found my groove (Yeah bay-bee). The people I was reading for seemed to enjoy my (as Veronica called it) 'dynamic' style. I become fully myself during readings and am a gregarious, say it like it is reader who usually make my clients laugh out loud and leave with a smile on their lips. Obviously I choose my moments and use a more discreet style with serious matters.

My senses were developing. I sensed and described deceased loved ones surprisingly accurately for clients yet at the time that was all. Until one day a regular client of mine who was also 'aware' announced that I didn't need the tarot cards and should be able to work without them (whimper. I love my cards and at the time considered them to be an extension of my left arm).

Lo and behold I found he was right. I just closed my eyes whilst in front of client and suddenly start seeing with my imagination (as They can work through your imagination – clairvoyance – to show you things). Eventually I just knew what the client felt and what was going on for them.

Now I just talk non-stop and occasionally use the cards on a 'not so tuned in' day. I am finding my cycles and the cycles of the moon affect my abilities as do many women who are psychic.

I found I was predicting future events, describing accurately past events, and seeing exactly the emotions the client was feeling that very moment. At first I wasn't aware of my accuracy, however a client or two would come back into the shop to find me as events had panned out as I had said. I would be gob smacked and embarrassed (believe it or not) to hear these accounts. I still have trouble saying that I have a tendency to hit the mark (see, I couldn't say accuracy. Dear dear) and really don't look to find out whether or not I was…..accurate. My only aim is to put a smile on people's faces or to put someone else's mind at ease. After that I would rather go home and have a cuppa with some chocolate (oops, did I say chocolate? Naughty me) and get lost in the usual routine of being a mum.

Life is relatively normal in our household and my son and I usually get on with life like the next person. (dirty socks and cat hair included)

'What does this have to do with Angels?' I hear you say. Well if you have a fair idea about my background you will understand that it is NORMAL to talk to Angels and accept their existence. That Angels are a part of our lives. Always have been but we just step around and past them as if they are not there. They don't mind and just allow you to continue on your way all the while whispering in your ear 'Watch out for the red light' or 'You are beautiful' or 'You are loved'. Hey, but that is limiting what they are truly able to do. They do so much more than whisper. They heal, defend (ooh that's a biggy. Just ask Arch Angel Michael), inform, educate and in this instance – communicate. Its Arch Angel Gabriel (Or so I believe) who will communicate through this book (I can't believe I just said that! I obviously I'm not taking him seriously hey?). As I said this is not my forte, writing books, but (sigh) as usual its 'jumping in the deep end' stuff. As you probably gathered there are spirit guides and deceased relatives, entities and of course Angels. This book is supposed to touch a little on each but mainly is driven towards the Angels.

We are all a big happy family. We just all don't know it yet. Guides are spirits who may have incarnated before. There are varying opinions of whether they are deceased relatives or other life time connections or if they are just spirits who may or may not have incarnated at all and are assigned you and me as helpers. My belief is that a guide is usually a spirit assigned to help us with their specialist skills. However I also believe deceased loved ones help and guide us in this way also but move on when their bit is done. They can choose to stay with you indefinitely or for one day.

Angels are a whole other book that I'm not remotely qualified to embark on. I am just writing about my experiences and interpret what poor Arch Angel Gabriel tries to tell me – a typical blonde – to tell you. Oi! What have I let myself in for?

Angels, as you probably know from other books, haven't incarnated on Earth. They have varying roles and different hierarchies. All that I know is that they are always around us and are forever ready to help us. We just literally have to ask. That has been said so many times before but I am going to try to elaborate. The Angels cannot interfere in our free will at all and unless an absolute dire emergency can't influence you or anyone else. They WANT to but can't. At least not until we wake up and smell the …… well you know what I mean. If we are being bullied and need guidance to avoid it then we have to literally say… "Please, Arch Angel Michael, can you protect me from ……." And if you wait and listen carefully you will get an answer. Such as a thought or idea to walk home from school a different way (even if it's the long way) that day and we find out that there was an ambush waiting at original route home. That may seem small but it still helped and that is how the Angels can help. They can work in more miraculous ways too and we will never know unless we open our hearts, minds and mouths to ask for help. Keep talking and interacting with them everyday. They adore you and are just as in awe of you as you are of them. They love you totally and await with bated breath your achievements and celebrate any successes. You have no idea what a part-ay goes on upstairs when you achieve your goals. Especially if it was on your list of 'to do's' and you did it! (Just had image of an over partied Angel with hangover).

We all have daydreamed, hey? And to try and do it now thinking of something which is of importance to you. Be it football or ballet, beer or chocolate, flowers or your kids. Try closing your eyes and imagine your daughter or son as if you're away in another city and miss them and are trying to imagine their faces and smell (by this I'm talking a scrubbed kid). Can you see the freckles on little Kate's face. Little Tom's missing two front teeth? Can you see the rich auburn hair of your husband or wife and how the colour is so close to that of a fine chestnut horse? The highlights of gold and copper with deeper tones of brown and bronze. This is how we intuitives see clairvoyantly the guides and sometimes Angels. This is the visual connection you can have with the others on the other side of the veil. This is the purpose of meditation. To help you develop your connection to spirit through your imagination with visualization. The other senses come along with it once you have that down pat. You act 'as if' the passed on loved ones are still around you. If you've ever experienced a ghost you'll have an idea of what 'feeling' those not still alive. It may feel like someone has come up behind you and without seeing them you just 'know' they are there. This is clairsentience, as is feeling an ache in your leg whilst you are standing next to your brother who has twisted his ankle. The ache should subside once you part ways.

Sometimes you swear someone whispered in your ear. You hear your name yet no-one is there to have uttered it. This is akin to clairaudience.

Then there are times where you just know how your loved one is feeling before they tell you. You just KNOW. This is akin to claircognizance.

Just close your eyes and imagine. Believe it or not there's a fine line between imagination and information that 'They' are trying to pass on to you. You USE your imagination to form these images. You may huff and puff saying it's too easy and that its hog wash but just try it and wait and see.

It's a game of absolute trust and faith. Both ways. Although 'Their' faith and trust in you never falters it's only us that doubt. To imagine your Angels just tune in (like a radio) and see what first comes to mind. Be open to anything. If he/she is wearing a fake beard then don't dismiss it as they have senses of humour too. It could be their way of lightening the mood. You don't have to see them though. You can sense them. Which, if you ask me, is more important. I usually experience a warm glowing sensation in the area of my heart. And a supported feeling coming from the solar plexus. This is when you just know how something is true or accurate. A lot of psychics sense things from their solar plexus chakra as it's the 'knowing' centre. We receive information there and is behind that old saying 'gut feeling' which describes how you feel when you are sure your hunch is right.

Right, now that I've briefly covered that perhaps you will understand a little how someone who is psychic (of which you are too) works. I have told you so you may try to visualise your Angels to. They have infused into my life the absolute love and adoration they have for me. I talk with them every day and will do so for the rest of my life. My life experiences have tested me and have forced me to lean on my Angels and in doing so has introduced me to the REALITY of which IS the Angelic world. They are so real that I have to sometimes walk around them to get to the toilet. They can be very 'In your face' and insistent. Especially when there is something they want me to do (Ha! Just look at what I'm doing!).

They work in subtler ways than we expect or demand of them. There have been reported visions of Angels scaring away would be attackers etc. But usually they just help by whispering in your ear the right thing to do or send you loving energy when you need the support. Its as simple as accepting it when it is given. Just because it doesn't come with a fanfare or fireworks doesn't mean the help isn't there. We have to do the hard yards I'm afraid as that is where the lessons are, but we are not alone. It's like our parents. You can pick up the phone to debrief with them but you have to do things on your own as you're probably old enough to. They probably want to help but you let's face it, if your over 18 then you need to take the bull by the horns and bite the bullet and do the hard yards yourself because you won't learn what you came here to learn. (Don't know if I could fit any more clichés into that sentence)

This is the same for your Angels. They can't live your life for you and can only guide you from where they are. My Angels don't show up with a neon sign strapped to their heads or orchestral music chiming every time they appear (even though this has been known to happen for some). It's usually in the subtle way I described earlier which outlines the visualisation methods I use. I close my eyes and tune in to the subtler realms. I become aware of my aura and with it I sense the Angelic energy around me and like the internet I download information from Them. Usually feelings more than visual as I find the feelings more accurate and appropriate for the moment. Any visuals I get are a bonus and can only add to it.

I feel them when I close my eyes and imagine them coming in close to me. I feel them just like I feel my son as if he was closing in on me, and feel the warmth of his body or energy he emits. I feel them as a warm tingly glow like the warmth of the sun and the warmth gradually warming me like the sun gradually peering out slowly from behind clouds. Once this feeling is achieved I then open up to sounds and sights in my mind's eye. I have found to be totally daring and acting 'as if' it is real, which it is but for the sake of explanation I'll pursue this description. Most of us are wary of behaving this way because of the rigid closed minded attitudes of those who are sceptic. To behave as if Angels are real is worthy of a stint in a mental hospital and most of the presumed gibberish we spiritual people speak is similar to that of a disturbed person. If you open up psychically too quickly and without proper preparation you can encounter things that can affect you but if you are stringent about what you believe and don't mess with darker versions of the occult you are very protected. However you must be responsible and careful. The methods I have touched on are to help you visualize your Angels not to delve into deeper realms of energy and psychic work. That is where you may need a reputable spiritualist church or psychic development group. And whatever you do have the common sense NOT to use a ouija board. It has got a bad reputation and most of that is due to what I was talking about before – being irresponsible. So BE RESPONSIBLE! and I usually imagine tree roots growing from my legs and feet well into the ground and feeling the sensation of being rooted to the spot. Also keep your chakras closed. Mainly your crown chakra. These are the energy centers all along your body. There are very good books out there on chakras but again it just depends on how far you wish to go with your intuitive explorations. This book won't go into depth about psychic development but I felt it needed touching upon just in case.

Arch Angel Gabriel is one of the four main known Arch Angels even though there are more. Gabriel is about communication. He brought the word of the birth to be of Jesus to Mary.

I call Him 'He' as that is how I experience Him. However many see Gabriel as a She. To roll out the old line, it doesn't matter as He/She is androgynous.

I usually work with and see Arch Angel Michael but that is for cleansing and protection. Gabriel is a lovely Angel to work with and stands back usually and lets my main Angels do their bit but sticks his head in when needed. Very compassionate and loving (as are all Angels) he has utmost love for all of us and can't wait to get started. I am busy writing this section of the book and he is dancing around in the background going 'Hurry up' as he is excited about talking to you. Yes YOU! Even as I write this I'm wondering how he intends to talk to you. I think it'll be through my intuition and 'imagination'. I will just work as I do for the people I read for. Will do my best to do his words justice (gulp).

I certainly aren't being arrogant saying Gabriel will talk through me because I am not looking for aggrandisement as I am naturally a very shy and private person. This is something I am being pushed to do. In a nice way. So I'm coming out of my comfort zone to do this. So here goes………..

To begin with I'll just let you know that there are 6 topics to be covered in this book that I was guided to jot down before I started and these are going to be at beginning of each chapter. I refer to God as He because that is easier than He/She.

"To inform those who are bereft of love that love still exists"

Good day my loved ones. I am here to tell you through my dear friend Lisa how to LOVE and be LOVED. Love is such a strong word and yet it needs to be in order for you to hear it.

Love is the only way to live and exist. It is the entire reason why we are here and is where we come from (everybody including Angels).

For those who yearn to feel Love need to turn their face to the sun who is the Father (pun not intended).

You know what it feels like. Even if you haven't received any Love in a while you will at least have a memory of it. That feeling of complete acceptance and support that a family and loved ones can give. By family and loved ones I mean those of whom are related to you or the adopted loved ones such as friends. It saddens me when I hear some of you have so little by way of love and support from biological loved ones. You are bereft of love through circumstances beyond your control. That despite your best intentions these people cannot love you the way you so desperately need and deserve. This is not to condemn those who do this to you as they have their own cross to bear. It is just not conducive to their life plan to express that at this time. Also they may be in pain and are stunted as to how to put it across. This is certainly not your fault. It is their lesson to learn how to express it and that is way beyond your control. All you can be responsible for is your own needs.

You forget my beloveds that WE are your loved ones. You may feel as uncomfortable about that as a child who is picked up by a stranger and hugged. They don't smell or feel the same and so you don't accept the hug on the physical or emotional levels. That is how it feels at first but if there has been a drought as far as loving touch and consideration are concerned you eventually warm to the person holding you and realise they are not different from you integrity wise. That is what we want you to feel with us. To allow us to be near to you and familiar to you. You forget that we have been with you always and forever. We have seen you go through many lifetimes with many different faces and yet you are still you to US. We wouldn't have it any other way.

You are so beautiful to us and we have raptures of love when we look into your eyes and souls. Not one single one of you is insignificant or worthless. Boy do we love you. You are God's creation as are we and the joy of that almost makes us giddy.

Imagine a child who knows nothing of wars or bullying or hatred or animosity. Who accepts with open arms whoever approaches them. This is what we want for you. This is how you can create love in your life. 'That is not practical in this day and age' I hear you say. 'Who says so?' I ask strongly. How come you're so cynical? Peer pressure is why and the physical world you live in can be harsh and people harden themselves to love. To them to show love is to show weakness. Not so, I say. To show love IS to be strong. To be like that child is how you're supposed to be. That does not mean you have to be ignorant or dismissive of the dangers out there but to live in cynicism and doubt is to completely limit your potential.

Go ahead and be that way but don't complain to us that life is hard and that we are robbing you of what is good and sweet in this world. You are responsible for that and whatever you feel bereft of in this circumstance you have contributed to.

Cynicism is phenomenological to man not Angels and we will take no part in pandering to those who practice it.

We are not judging you or rejecting you. We just want you to realise you are responsible for you.

Of course We want to speak of those who have hardship which is beyond their control. These people are a different category all together and will be addressed thusly. You cannot blame yourselves for others abuse. You did make life choices before you incarnated however you may still be doing it tough and need reassurance. You did not deserve the hardship, you chose it on one level. Nobody deserves hardship but it is a tool with which you realise your strengths. You are deserving of more. We Angels attend to those with hardships with the loving attention it requires and whisper to you positive ideas and thoughts. We buoy you through poverty, hunger and depression. You think you can't feel us but why have such little faith in yourself? You won't be ridiculed for believing in us. If it helps don't talk about us. Just keep us private within your heart. You may feel we have deserted you. Do you know how that belief holds you back? Go ahead, sulk and refuse to talk to us. You will be limiting yourself not us. We may sound harsh but it is a measure of how much we love you. You may know it as 'Tough Love'.

Some leave it to the very last, dire moment to call on Us and our Father. There is never a time that this is ignored. If that is the way it is to be so be it! We could have helped sooner but you had to go through a process to get to where you finally recognised us and asked.

We judge you not. We are always here and never ever will we leave.

We are minimalists. We don't believe in frivolities nor do we humour people. We say what we have to say and leave you with it. Do with it what you will.

Your beloved guides are with you and we urge you to use them. See it as a partnership like those of your workmates. They are perfect for helping you because they were and still are close to you. They may have been your loved ones or friends and who better to help you with your life dreams than them?

We Angels are what some would call 'The Big Daddies' of help. We intervene at most urgent of times and yet respect your free will. We can give the most help when it is beyond the capacity of your guides.

Sometimes it seems you have forgotten us and where you came from. We are all family regardless of what you call us and how can family refuse you?

You identify yourself with your physical family and feel like you would betray them to even entertain the idea that others could be your family too.

Why, they are our family also so what's the difference?

We laugh along with you when you giggle at something. We bask in your joy like a kitten does when you scratch him under the chin. There is a joy in that, no? We lap up that energy too. Not in a leech like way but in a sharing way. We want to share our warmth with you for it is in these moments you are truly yourself and then some of you recoil and return back to your comfort zone. This saddens us because it dims your light to us. No-one wants to see a child laugh then withhold that laugh for fear of judgement. We want them to be uninhibited and we protect that in our children. If they are having trouble at school fitting in and stop laughing because of timidity or someone jeering at them then we fight for their right to laugh for that is showing who they really are. The pure energy of joy that they are an expression of. This is what We want for you. We are so integral to your happiness in this way. We fight for your right to be who you really are and to make you realize you are far more than what others make of you. Laugh like a child. Live like a child. LOVE like a child. Who says children are wrong to act as they do? How dare they limit another by telling them to hold it in. We are not correct to impose on another how they should act. Those who criticise a joyful person are really those who are so rigid and inflexible and stuck in a limited paradigm. They are not to be hated as they are lost children themselves.

These people are like the ones who reject the notion of spirituality and Angels and such. They are the ones who are sceptical and deem themselves to be in the 'Real World'. Bah humbug!' We say.

They see us as limited and ungrounded. Imbalanced if you will. They probably have a very cynical view about love too. With this attitude they won't attract love and if they do then they won't know how to keep it or maintain it. Or even acknowledge that they have it until its too late. They have closed themselves off from love and withhold feelings and emotions. This is no way to be. Dear, dear. It is so sad to see Our loved ones do this to themselves for it is really those who do this who are limited and imbalanced. This type of behaviour leads to the needing of your psychologists and counsellors. Of course we love them equally as much as any other but we have to say it as it is as this is only way someone will know that they are 'disconnected'. Those of you who 'get' what We say are connected. Not better than, just connected. Those who think this is rubbish are disconnected. They just are. It's not a judgement or criticism.

If they truly were connected then they would feel love. They would know love. They would express and articulate love. They would BE love.

These people who claim to be realists and yet shun Angelic help and laugh at those who don't are in and of themselves bereft of love. This is no way to be. It is done because of fear but mostly because of experience of pain. We all experience pain at some point in our lives but some earlier than others. Those who shut us out and others too are the ones who have experienced pain and have not realized We are here to help. They say that miracles didn't happen to protect them that We didn't save them. So they shun us and push us away in an act of anger and feeling of worthlessness. That if they were worthwhile someone or something would have stepped in to stop it. And withdraw in disgust at the spirit world and swear to never again put their faith in them. They discard the belief that there is a God because He didn't stop the abuse or pain inducing occurrences so He doesn't exist. This is what we mean by turning away from the light of God.

To not love another, to not love yourself is to not love the God energy within you. You may do this because of lack of self-worth and from being rejected. All you need is to find your way home to Us. Oh how we want to hold you and take your cares away. We can't because you won't let us. You believe you have to do it yourself probably because you're in survival mode. And no, letting Us in is not leaving you wide open and vulnerable. We are not human so We don't have the capacity nor motive to betray. It's not in Our vocabulary. It is only your attributing human qualities onto Us that holds you back not Us doing that to you.

Trust is the key. Faith too. Trust is the act of Love. Love is the act of Trust. Those who reject us have no faith or trust and have learnt to navigate through life that way because it's a means to an end. It gets them what they need, or is that what they THINK they need. Meanwhile We are sitting patiently waiting for these lost souls to realize the existence of God and the Angels. We haven't lost faith or trust. We know it's only a matter of time before they come back to us. After all they are going round in 'safe' circles and if they are to get ANYWHERE they are going to finally realize that the only way to do so is to live in the light of God. That is live in Love. Love brings you anything. With love you feel like you can do anything you put your mind to. Which, of course, you can. You are restricted only by what you are programmed to believe is possible. Guess what? You can reprogram yourself, or better yet let God do it for you. The God We mention is non-denominational. Only you create religion the way it exists on Earth today. You misunderstand and under-estimate God and His word so often. We are not angry with you in saying this, just informing you that all is not as it seems and that although religion has its benefits and comforts it is also a human interpretation of God's word. Each of you need to experience God in your own way. Someone else's experience is their own. Not different or wrong but personal.

No matter what you do or say love still exists and We love you no matter what. Love is the energy through which we experience God. God wants us to experience him for in doing this we can transform like a chrysalis to a butterfly. The energy flow increases once you are in tune. This is akin to driving a car too close to the edge of the road and slowing down due to the gravel then straightening up and back onto the tarmac which is smoother and with less drag. Once back on the road it's smoother and suddenly faster. You get to your destination quicker. Colourful analogy We know but you get Our drift. When on the right path your travelling is smoother and more efficient. So too when you commune with God and the Angels. It is on this path where you rediscover yourself and the self-love will grow. It is then that you get the true meaning of what and who God is. People who talk in spiritual speak all know what each other says as if it is another language. What a wonderful way to perceive it. For that is what it almost is. Those of you who scratch your heads and even sneer at what is being said act as if these people are talking double dutch. If you're in the know none of it will be nonsense to you. This is not to say that those who 'get it' are better than or more worthy than those who don't, it's just that they are waiting for the others to catch up. Those who find it perplexing have yet to find their way. That's OK it's all growth. There are things along the way these souls are to pick up and learn from that will help keep it in context. They can't just fast track to spiritual enlightenment as it would be a complete overload. All is perfect in creation and the order in which it happens.

There is a process that each and every one of you have to go through and for some that includes being bereft of love and lonely. There is a longing these people have for that which others have. There is a reason why one of the Commandments said Do not covet. Not because God was going to strike you down with a streak of lightning but because it causes the person 'without' a lot of stress and disconnects them from the God energy through losing self-worth. To be bereft of love is to believe that there is no love. For them at least. Something in their life has led them to feel that such a thing as love just does not exist. Or if it did it lives somewhere else now. That they don't deserve it. Why else would they be without. They feel unlovable and unwanted. Someone is possibly withholding love or abusing them. We are saddened by this and try as we might we try to imbue our support through sensory means. Such as a warm glow in the heart area which lifts them long enough to feel self-acceptance and self-love in order to make more appropriate life decisions. THIS is how we work. In a subtler way than expected. We leave the dramatic entrances for emergencies. This can happen briefly but if its life saving then it's worth it. Who needs trumpets and booming kettle drums when We can get the best results purely from subtlety and sweet gentle caresses. That is why belief is so important and integral to Our process. As soon as someone believes it makes it so much easier to move through trials. If you lack belief then troubles bottleneck and you get a backlog of issues that need attending to. This then feeds self-doubt and perpetuates the perceived void of lack of love. You limit yourself. This is not an accusation or harsh criticism, it's just saying it like it is so you can wake up sooner and see the sunrise. Please don't limit yourself. Don't 'Hide your light under a bushell'. There is something to be said for wisdom. Well, a lot actually as We are sure you agree. When to speak or not to speak. When to make a move and when not to move. When to love and when not to love. There is wisdom in not being frivolous with love. Being discerning with who you love is wise. To withhold love can be an act of self-protection. This does not mean to stop loving but containing it wisely as some situations calls for us to be cruel to be kind. Such as breaking up from a relationship. You can still love that person but contain it enough in order to let that person go if your time together is up. To keep on loving in an extreme way will cause you disruption and more heartache. Loving someone enough to let them go and be free because that is what they want is wise. Purely because you are helping yourself to categorize that emotion and assimilate the lessons in it. It's not just about the other party. It's about how it affects you and how you allow it to affect you.

There are those who can't let go of love. Or what they believe is love. This is hard to do they think and continue with the charade because of fear of being alone with themselves, heaven forbid! What is so bad to be with yourself? You who are an expression of love incarnate. Yes you are, don't argue with us!

What else could you be? You believe that you deserve rejection, that you are lower than dirt. You have no rights and will never be loved. This is a very painful way to exist don't you think? Why, We ask, do that to yourself? Especially when the energy you use to feel this way and perpetuate this construct could so easily be channelled into more promising and practical potentials. Love isn't given out without just cause by God. You are very loved by Him and you are worthy of it.

If love isn't working and it's causing pain then it becomes something other than true love. True love shows no restrictions and allows freedom of speech and thought. If you are feeling paralysed or stuck and even sad within a relationship then you cannot possibly be your true self. You become what you think the other person expects of you. It's not about what they DO think about you its about how YOU interpret it. One thing, don't assume anything of another. Because of this some feel they can't let go. It's akin to the feeling of letting go of a branch as you hang over a ravine. If you let go you fall into an abyss. A bottomless pit with no relief. So you cling to what you think will keep you feeling alive. The unknown is scary and awe inspiring. It causes us to freeze and put up with what we already have.

Look at a child. A child is closer to her maker than an adult. A child survives naturally in a love bereft environment by accepting their circumstances, some even developing relationships with invisible friends (or are they?). There are severe environments that some children live through where the only source of love is from within themselves and even that is threatened. We Angels hold these dear little beings even closer and We find the connection with these little ones is stronger because the use of intuition just purely for survival is used knowingly or unknowingly. These children grow up to become very aware. By this we mean not only intuitively but also interpersonally. They have spent most of their lives watching and observing human nature. Mainly in order to predict when it's safe to just be. They may be perceived as damaged goods by someone's twisted outlook (by twisted We mean distorted) however We see them as little ones (or not so little) with great character and love within them. We could learn from them how to self-love. Even THEY may not be aware we have such faith as this in them. They may feel that they are worthless and hateful. Not at all. They show that they still love their persecutors enough to protect them enough by taking the blame. Never thought of it that way did you? No matter if it looks dysfunctional. It shows that out of dire circumstances love still exists. These little ones have no other weapon left other than love to keep themselves afloat. We admire them for being brave enough to dare to live a life of hardship. From the darkest depths springs forth the tiniest germination of a seed of love. And from this it can only grow upward toward the light of God. He who is all that there is!

Why doubt it? It takes more energy to doubt than to believe. Bit like it takes more muscles in your face to frown than to smile. So smile because the cavalry is here. We sound like We joke but how good is it to pass on information than in a humorous way?

Wouldn't you prefer to laugh than to be sad? We are not comedians and have a serious message to get across but levity alleviates a topic that can be very heavy.

We are trying to demonstrate how to turn a negative into a positive.

Love shows itself through the word and communication, proper communication is an act of love. For those who use the word lightly without much thought for those they are dumping on can create pain. Regardless of whether it was intentional or not it blocked the feeling of love. To have the mind to stop yourself mid-sentence and take responsibility for what you say is an act of love.

Love does exist in many disguises and one of them is thoughtful communication. To express to someone enlightening information, information which will make life easier for them, is done from love. The person expressing this information cares enough to consider the other party and their needs and rights.

We are so proud of you when you do this. It shows growth and development in the right direction. We do not condemn those who forget to do this. We merely wait for them to catch on. It's not that those who are perceived as mean or deficient are devoid of love. It's just that they have lost connection and need to switch it back on just like a light switch. They are, in effect, in a darkened room and are fumbling to find the switch. They lash out because of fear and anger at tripping over in the darkness. It's too painful to look at what it is within them that is causing this so they externalise it.

They don't hate you. It's themselves whom they hate. Hate is a strong, strong word. Dislike might be more sensitive. All of human kind is capable of love. However those who are in their head more are the ones who don't show it. To be angry or full of ire are thinking more than feeling. This is because they have had to rely on their cognitive processes more because it is seen as more credible and also to survive in a world that esteems the mind more than the heart. They have not been able to balance the head with the heart which will keep their emotions on an even keel. The message has been to watch what you think because it influences the outcome and that the heart in turn influences thoughts. So the perceived message is to disconnect the head from the heart and rely totally on the head. If you feel and allow yourselves to be sentient beings then it opens us to empathy which to some detracts from what it is THEY want. To fear giving at the risk of not receiving in return is a major problem and potentially causes lack and the inherent pain that goes with it.

As that old saying goes 'Nothing ventured, nothing gained'. You need to venture out emotionally from behind that metaphorical couch and brave the emotional world. Love is such a wonderful feeling and We highly recommend it. Like a fine wine, it can only get better. As can making love. With love present the act of sex can only explode into rapture.

Some even say they 'cook with love'. Never underestimate that statement. Cooking with love is a way someone shows their love for another. Just ask your parents. But more of that in another chapter.

Lisa: Thankyou Gabriel for your wonderful words.
I look forward to the next chapter.

Gabriel: With blessings my lovely child. You are loved beyond measure and we appreciate this opportunity to work with you in this way.

"How to see love. The many ways it is sent and received"

Greetings my loved ones. Talking to you like this is so sweet. It is as it should be. Always. We so long to hear your voices and this opportunity to do so was eagerly grasped for because it means you hear us and seek us out. We are ecstatic and overjoyed. It is a state in which We revel as often as We can because it is a lovely feeling. Again like the purring cat who is being scratched under the chin. It is your act of listening to us that satisfies us. It is demonstrative of your connectedness. Yes Our loved ones, YOU are now connected and We say welcome.

The very act of picking up this book and reading what is within it means you are connected. Even more so if you understand everything We say. Be open to what is discussed herein and We will promise to lift your heart.

Our intention is just that and in no way do We mean for you to feel hurt or criticized by what We say. We discuss examples of negative occurrences purely to show contrast and explain the positives. We do not ever judge you or accuse you of being less than what you should be. We only want to throw light upon God's grace and the path you can take to reach him. He is not a deity whom is inaccessible or unreachable. Don't you see sweet ones, He IS love. When you love you are joining in the act of connecting with God. That is what it is all about. Coming home to Him. It is not 'double dutch' as We said before and is not that hard to grasp. You just have to want to do so. Come, just put your hand in Our's and trust We will take care of you.

We see the love in you, all that is needed is that you see the love in you. Love is an energy form. That is why We talk about it all the time.

We are not just talking fancy talk or as you call it 'mumbo jumbo'. There is a method to the madness. It's the language of love we speak that those who are connected will understand. It's an energy exchange and God and love are one and the same. To love means you will also receive it. It's a fair exchange. Not conditional or open to bribes. To love totally is to love purely and to not taint it with the human trait of being conditional. To deny the love within you is to deny the God energy within you. If you do this how is it possible to love another? Don't withdraw from God and love, for others will suffer. We don't mean to alarm you or accuse you of a heinous crime. We know you are beautiful and worthy of love. We see you when you demonstrate love. We are just showing you what the lack of it does to others around you. If you withdraw from love (and God) then you lose the connection to empathy. It is with empathy that you feel for others around you. To FEEL opens the door to love and its benefits. When you feel empathetic towards someone you are then able to see how much you do love them. Then it is when you realise you are in the act of loving. To be aware that is what you are doing is when you become alert to the possibility of a God. When in the act of LOVE you are making yourself susceptible to awareness and belief in God. Those who have trouble with the concept of God are the ones who, if they DO love deeply their loved ones, don't connect the dots. That in doing so(connecting the dots) they become connected to God. If you are aware of love then the likelihood of becoming aware of the connection between it and God is greater. To accept love yet reject the idea of a God is an oxymoron. You can't have one without the other. It's just that these people can't see it. They don't see any physical proof of it so it can't be so. And any attempts to get them to see it prove futile as they are not looking for it in the right way. The sensitive new age person's way of seeing the connection is fobbed off and dismissed. 'We need hard solid facts!' they say. Well you'll be waiting indefinitely We say as We don't perform tricks to suit. We are not show ponies or hired entertainment. We have no need to prove it to you.

The act of being calm and in your centredness with trust and faith (there's those words again) and living each day as it comes will get you closer to feeling Us.

The people who believe in God and the Angels are confident that We exist and don't feel the need to prove it. Some would snigger at that and call these wonderful, loyal souls 'suckers'. Being the way that these loyal souls are is actually more cluey than any doubter. They are not blinded by their faith. They are not gullible. They are not boring. They are good people trying to live in your world as best they can and using a formula for creating a happy, love filled life and one without stress. Stress happens when there is a perceived lack. Note the word perceived. Go ahead and 'perceive' you have no love. You are obviously a glutton for punishment. It's a very self-absorbed person who believes that they are right to sulk because they have no physical love in their life. Stop wasting yours and Our time and wake up and be real. We are talking to those who think they have a lack not those who are in an abusive situation. There are those who can't help it and then there are those who can. It is the latter that we are addressing. We have addressed the former in the previous chapter. We have no problem with them.

Love can be found wherever you look. Wherever God has touched there is love. Be it in nature, or in man-made structures. Those who create huge buildings which house departments that take care of the poor and needy have helped in the act of God and the act of love, no matter how indirect it seems. Nurses and doctors are called angels of mercy. This is not to be taken lightly and believe Us when We say that We agree. To save another's precious life is an indirect act of God. This is not to say a heart surgeon is God as this would be wrong. But to be a passionate physician who's only drive is to keep others alive and well is acting as God wants all of us to do. God works through us when we are passionate and devoted. He is parental in his disposition. Not to make you less significant or subservient but to make you feel loved and cherished, safe and protected. It is a role He is happy to take. He wants to guide you to finding the real you and for you to realise your goals.

Sometimes, though, you are not looking in the right places and get frustrated and then throwing your hands up in the air forsaking God and sinking deep into a depression. We dance around waving and hollering (most undignifying don't you think for an Angel?) trying to get your attention.

It's like Lisa. We see her struggle just a little while ago with self-acceptance and love. Even as We write this book she struggles. She understands and agrees with fully the concepts We put forth but her own inner voice is forever apologizing for her existence. We talked with her and she found that her convictions were along Our lines but was fighting her inner programming. She's been programmed to take the blame and criticism because she has to. Or so she feels. It defies her logic and she knows it. She is normally a happy, carefree person but has to literally beat off this set way of thinking with a stick.

This leads us to the saying you have 'God helps those who help themselves.'

To expect God to step in and just intervene whenever life gets complicated and difficult defeats the purpose of why you are here. God and We Angels want you Our children to fight the good fight and live your lives. God cannot live it for you. When you realise it's not that hard or at least as hard as you made out, then you get on with it you will be closer to feeling God.

As the saying goes He helps those who help themselves. This is not conditional and saying that He won't help you unless you do something for him. It is an energy exchange of which has a logic to it. When you're in THE ZONE where you are facing your fears and 'biting the bullet' so to speak, you are closer than ever to God's plan for you. You are thinking and behaving as God intended you to do. Bravely and with faith. And if you behave with faith you are having faith in guess who – God. So you are communing with God and having a relationship with him.

He is waiting to offer you a helping hand but you can't expect him to come all the way. You need to meet him in the middle. The reason for this is if God did everything for you you would end up with no life skills. Just like your children. Do you think it's fair if they expect you to pick up clothes off the floor which is obviously their responsibility to do? No. You know if that goes on for much longer you'll be doing it until they are 21. 'That is not on.' I can hear you say. Then so it is for God and the Angels. That is not to say We have left you. Especially if you have REAL hardship and are battling bravely on. However if your trials are well within your capacity to cope with then you need to stop crying and help yourself. It's very parental We know but it is meant with love. And here We are full circle back at that word – LOVE.

How perfectly just. Appropriate. Considering what this book is about. No matter what route you take it all comes back to Love. You come from love and you will return to love. This is what Lisa hasn't quite grasped yet. That she IS love and comes from it so how could she possibly be worthless. When we are young we are in an environment which moulds us into who we are today. It's a combination of our family's beliefs and the beliefs of others around us such as our peers, and also our own beliefs which are shaped according to how we perceive and experience the world as we live in. There is a ripple effect within a family unit. Whatever dysfunction there is can be passed down generation to generation. We call this 'dysfunction' but it isn't as severe as it sounds. It's just a way to describe disconnection from God. For when you are disconnected from God your behaviour becomes less God-like. You hurt others or yourself by resisting your destiny and role. By 'role' We don't mean to hem you in and control how you are, We mean the role YOU chose to enact in this life time. You did, after all, have a say in what was charted to happen in this incarnation. The message We try to tell Lisa and now you is that nothing is wrong. Not one thing you choose to do is wrong. But because you are torn in two regarding decision making and are forced to make a choice you mourn the one you didn't make. This is energy wasted. Make your choice, stick to it and don't regret. You can do the other one the next time round. There is no wrong choice. What you choose is what you choose. No more no less. To mourn the one that you didn't opt for causes the stress and the urge to OVER control does too. What is the point in this We ask? For if you had chosen the other one you'd be in the same boat but the other way around.

Now to get back to the topic at hand. 'How to see Love'

Love, as We have described, can be seen in your behaviour towards others. And in theirs to you. Love can be seen in the way you receive other's behaviour. If someone lashes out at you unreasonably because they're in pain and you take it calmly so as not to inflame and create any more pain, this shows you are capable of great love. For in love is great understanding and compassion. This is an intelligent thing to do. Have understanding and compassion that is. It shows that you have the connection We keep mentioning. Next time you find this happening to you remind yourself that this is a demonstration of love for another. Not for self-aggrandisement as We are sure you're aware, but to start finding ways to see love.

Love is wonderful to receive and experience but boy is it great to give. Especially when you see the response to it and how it leaves you feeling.

It's a gift to the giftee and the giver (it's corny but humour us). To give to another is an act of love because your aim is to make someone happy – because you care. This comes from love.

To receive is to realise you are loved and in turns into joy – which IS love. Are you with Us?

The child We have talked about before is an example of joy. Children are naturally joyful. They tap into it at a drop of a hat. It's like they live on pure joy. They see it in everything. Which is why they bounce around when their parents come home from work. They innocently look forward to Mother or Father's return. Innocence is a key word. We Angels profess to working with innocence ourselves. It allows a purer channel through which We can work. We wish to lead by example and work this way to show how to do so yourself. But many of you feel the need to be 'worldly' or cynical. Not to mention sceptical and wary. This is very limiting and it holds you back from exploring many other potentials. It's also arrogant to think you are above this. And to think you know better than God.

Who do you think created you? Never try to second guess Him up above. Or feel that you're on to Him. He knows all and sees all way before you do and is in constant flux of creation.

When you realize, at long last, that EVERYTHING comes from love only then can you relax and trust and go with the flow. Have you ever noticed how these sceptics and cynics are not relaxed or at ease. They are proud of being on alert and in a state of readiness. Espousing how nothing gets past them. Now is that any way to live We ask you? This stems from fear. What else can We say? Fear causes a lot of problems in your society. It's disguised as bravado and daring not to mention laughter. It is a sign of instability. Instability and fear come from a lack of love. These people cannot see the qualities in love as more beneficial to them than shrewdness and cunning.

When one is in love one sees everything in vivid colour. Everything is magical and special. One's energy is lifted and you have butterflies in your tummy.

Nothing is impossible in your love struck eyes. And why should it be? For that is how many a challenge has been successfully surmounted. Love equals passion and vis versa. For if you are passionate you can accomplish a great deal and overcome any challenge. And if that is the case then Love conquers all.

This is where you find love, in what it is you're passionate about. Be it a person or work, hobby or cause. A child of whom you adore. Imagine their little glowing face and their big saucer like eyes. How they open their arms to hug you without question or condition. Doesn't it fill your heart with glee. That warm glow in your heart and that swelling sensation of pride and – dare We say it – LOVE!

Too saccharine for you? Why, how cynical. If it is this to you then you're welcome to put down this book and go about your business. Trust Us, We'll meet again.

Now for those who are still with us let's get down to business.

We mention love continuously because to Us just saying the word brings us raptures of joy and bliss. To attain this state is highly recommended and We wish for you to experience it which is why We try to explain the many ways it is used and seen. How can you not enjoy talking or feeling about love? It's like your addiction to chocolate. You can never have enough.

Those who know what we are talking about appreciate it and are not afraid to explore it from every angle. Those who love freely know that you can never tire of talking about it as it validates their experience of it.

Love is like a drug, albeit a safe one. It raises you up high and elevates your spirits and even, so We believe, is good for you physically! Now can you see why We rave about it?

A nun is a living example of devotion which stems from her love for God. She asks no questions and goes about her business 'obeying' God and is perfectly joyous in doing so. Perhaps it is the simplicity of her love that sustains her. She doesn't have the complexities of modern, materialistic life. The need to have the best clothes, cars, wine or social network. She has all the basics catered for and has bypassed the need to fill her life with superficial and materialistic requirements. She has found that love still exists even without jewellery or perfumes. No need for cliques or social standing. She is free to express love in the purest of ways she knows how. Abstinence and piety are a requirement and clears a lot of the clutter that can cause stress and fear. She has an inbuilt support system in her fellow sisters, and of course God. To clear your life of the man-made complexities and live a very simple, uncluttered life frees your life up to concentrate on one thing and in doing so magnifies it until it imbues totally into your life. She is love in motion. Those nuns who work in third world countries love unconditionally. Which is how it should be for all of you. To see past the racial differences and just get on with the job at hand is love in action. To live in service to others is what you all should do. It is what you were designed to do. God created man in his likeness and it is more than just physical. You are a three dimensional expression of God's love.

Positive affirmations are designed to help you get back into thinking in a God-like manner. To find a paragraph in a favourite book that seems to say a lot of which you can relate to it makes sense to have it written down and stuck to your fridge. It's a positive act of self-love to find reminders of how to think in constructive and happy ways.

Like that favourite uncle who pulls coins from behind your ears or keeps stealing your nose with his fingers. He is full of mirth and mischief. But after he leaves you feel happy and full of fun and miss him until his next visit. You grow in excitement as his next visit approaches and from the moment he walks in the door and ruffles your hair you realise you appreciate the carefree and jolly soul who gets complete pleasure in making you smile. This person has tapped into his God source. That purest part of himself which is love and joy and has the foresight to share it and make others life wonderful to experience. He could be akin to a physical version of a positive affirmation. A constant reminder of how to find your bliss. To find your centre, your wholeness and YOUR God-source. To always see the funny side of life. For how better a way to express love than with laughter. Which is evident in the amount of jokes the aforementioned Uncle may tell you.

Positive affirmations can pin point and capture the true essence of a moment. It can put into words motivational ideas which spur you on to achieve things you never before imagined you would. The people who wrote these affirmations are clear in their understanding of life and are steadfast in their beliefs. They are providing a clue as to how to act with love. To act with love is to live to your fullest. To act with love means you are connected to Our Father. To act with love means you are on your true path. Positive affirmations try to help you do this. To see that you're not a bad person and that We have faith in YOU. For We sometimes influence the authors of these affirmations.

So as you can see, love can be seen in the written form.

Many a book has been written on love and God, Oh and Us Angels too. We love it when We get the opportunity to speak with you through this medium. It feels like a reunion at the airport between long lost family members. You know you belong to them inherently but have been parted from them for a lifetime and so there is a breathtakingly exhilarating moment where you recognise them and realise you are not alone and that now you DO belong. Then you pause before you embrace them. The mind assessing from conditioning to doubt or be wary. But then emotion takes over all reason and overflows into your heart and the floodgates open allowing the final embrace. Then you pull away to soak up how they look and to see the resemblances. This compounds the final outcome of evidence of belonging. Of opportunities for being loved unconditionally. This happens quite a bit in the physical world but try to entertain it as a metaphor for how you discover Us. Either through prayer or even through the written word. Which is eagerly looked forward to by us. To be able to speak and positively affect you through the books we channel with blessed souls like Lisa (Oh she has trouble with us saying that. We urge her to write it despite her fears of being judged by you for being narcissistic. Of which she isn't. Otherwise We wouldn't be working through her).

We hope that you find clarity by reading this book. And to find more meaning in your lives. To understand that We are here and are as real as the person sitting next to you on the bus. We only want to share our outlook. Hoping it will be contagious and rub off onto you. Especially if you are down and 'bereft of love'.

Think of an azure blue sky. The depth of colour that surrounds you. It stretches as far as the eye can see. The colour is rich and vivid and makes your heart sing as you look around and see how green the grass is and how alive the people or animals around you are. You appreciate God's world of creation.

Then there's the joy of a good tome. You get lost in fiction of which is yet another form of creation. Or perhaps you enjoy biographies because you like getting inside other people's heads as it gives you insight into your own thoughts and precepts. This brings us back to passion. Some express their passion by painting the blue sky and the green grass. Some in writing books. Others in playing music. Oh, how We love music and its way of getting our message across. Music is such a form of creation that taps directly into emotion and yet is very cerebral in its structure. We talk, of course, classical music. However ALL music is expressive and useful to Us and Our message. Whatever tickles your fancy (bear with Us, We are working within the boundaries of Lisa's quirky vocabulary).

The bands of your era were definitive of what messages YOU wanted to parlay. Their songs made you laugh, cry, sing along and dance. There are songs that define an era. Ones that you make love to. And importantly, ones you get married to. There is a reason why you have music at weddings and that is to raise the emotions. To experience fully the climactic moment which is your union. It helps to convey your feelings of love for one another to those around you so you may share the joy you feel and in doing so is an act of sharing and of love. You are so blissfully happy at this point in your life that you want all to feel what you feel. Its ceremonial and gatherings of people since time immemorial have celebrated life, death and marital unions in order to get closer to their God. As a way of experiencing that holy sensation of love everlasting through their loved ones getting married. Man has a habit of living vicariously through others and it is how he experiences emotions he may not otherwise feel. Man loves to feel emotions which are positive and if someone is celebrating a happy occasion in their lives than others around them join in to be able to partake of the joy that comes from their loved ones excitement. Love and joy are infectious and any excuse to vicariously experience this is usually seized. Why not? This is an opportunity for them to join in and contribute to the ecstasy and bliss of the joyful celebration.

This is why man has had pagan ceremonies for many years. The ceremonies raise energies that can be channelled into positive outcomes. Prayer is a more commonly known way to connect with God and many a wise woman or man will know that to call on the help of their God through ceremony and/or prayer gets them into the zone where they can raise energy to channel in order to heal and to help circumstances. All you ever have to do to get what you want (within reason) is pray and ask your Maker or Us Angels. We are not 'Father Christmas' and cannot supply on demand material goods or miracles. That is not to say miracles don't exist. Just the attitude of 'expecting' us to jump will not get a response. Believing We will help you, having faith and trust We will help you when asked is different in attitude. This is more appealing to Us Angels. You wouldn't like it if someone was rude enough to EXPECT you to jump when called so why should We?

Only when We are asked with a tone of gratitude and a real necessity do We step in and help. It is not intended with arrogance or haughtiness. It's the energy exchange thing again. If We receive a request in a pleasant tone then We feel pleasant and want to reciprocate. Just like you do when you're asked to do or get something. If someone is demanding then they haven't learnt their lessons. They need to be gently forced by Us Angels to learn to have trust which in turn quells the impatience and makes them have faith in us to deliver what is required when it is required and when We deem it necessary. Don't misunderstand Us. We are not being harsh or judgemental. We merely want you to realise that We want only the best for you and for it to happen to you with the right timing. We are not being petulant or stubborn. It is you that can be stubborn. What We do is very simple yet firm in its delivery. Being firm with a loved one can be an act of love because it is in their best interests.

We want you to see the love in Our actions and not focus on the lack. Optimism, not pessimism, cultivates the aura of love and from this comes love and its outer manifestation. To see love in its many forms means you are open and optimistic as opposed to closed minded, rigid and stubbornly pessimistic. All you need to be is open to it and to not limit yourself. Allow your thoughts lead to love and all the ways you see it manifest in the world around you. It is not a silly, futile and frivolous act. Only those who are sceptics see it this way and basically are going round in circles looking for love and yet not finding it. We wonder why? Perhaps opening their eyes and looking would help. Better yet open their hearts!

These people don't or can't or even won't see love in its true light. They may think they have it but We say that they can open up even more to it by believing. By this We mean their existing relationships may contain 'love' but due to the person's lack of belief and abundance of scepticism they don't realise that they have room to open up even more to more profound and fulfilling love. It may be love in a form that they can't see, which is why they are doubters in the first place, but who's to say it doesn't FEEL real.

There are millions of people who feel it and they belong to more mainstream religions and belief systems. They bask in the glory of God and the feeling of love is palpable.

Love is reinforced greatly within organised religion when they receive 'signs' from above. These signs are seen as miracles and bring elation to scores of people who look for signs that their faith is as strong as ever.

Some would say these people are fools and that these miracles can be explained. We say does it really matter. It's done its job and that is to reinforce faith and love. It should be of no consequence to detractors and those of whom do believe have profound emotions due to the miracle. Guess what? They are seeing something within the miracle. A sign. They see a sign of LOVE. And isn't that the whole point of miracles? It's certainly the whole point of this chapter.

It is perceived as a sign from God. And who's to say it isn't? We know it's real and We don't feel the need to prove it's real. It is what it is. And if the result is a mass acceptance of love then it has achieved its aim. Why can't people just accept that it's a display to evoke love. Surely that is a good thing? Heaven knows you need all you can get whilst having your Earthly experience.

It all depends on how you see it. The people who witness a miracle certainly don't see it as a con. The only conflict they would have would be if some busy body whispered in their ear that it's a hoax. Why do you always question God and Us Angels? Don't you see YOU are causing the conflict not Us and definitely not God. Your cynicism is like a toxin. You would be what is known in your world as a 'party pooper'.

Love is an important ingredient to your survival. So relish whatever morsel that comes your way. There will never be a real lack just a perceived one. But the motion of seeing love and believing there is love is enough to sustain you. See love in everything around you just like God intended. Just know it exists. A child sees it in you and whoever they come across. This beautiful child of God has not yet been conditioned and feels free to act out of love and to see love in who and whatever they come across. If this child can do this, and remember you were one once too, then surely you can see love too. It's not as hard as you think. Just act 'as if'. Be open to it and look for it. Sit like in meditation and look all around you. If you're in a bus station observe they young couples in love and watch them holding hands and gaze into each other's eyes. Do they seem aware you're watching. No? Well isn't that a surprise. Goes to show how powerful love is.

There may be a young mother with a child on her lap. Look at how she strokes the child's cheek in a loving way. We show love through physical actions as well as through our eyes and voice. The young mother was using all three to sooth her little one. It is because she loves that she does so.

Love comes in many forms and it is up to us to find them. So We urge you – keep looking. Half the fun is in the looking. We will whisper in your ear as you go and We will celebrate when you find it. For when you find it you will find Us. You will be as one with God. Boy what a joyous experience that will be.

"How Angels are integral to Love's delivery"

Well you could say this one is easy. And it is. Obviously sitting reading this book right now can answer that question. We have chosen to speak through Our loved Lisa in order to deliver the message of Love.

We are working on many levels towards this goal and one level is to help you and another is to help Lisa. She is learning as We work through her to write what is within this tome. Many a time We smile as We see the expression on her face of surprise and laughter when she types something that touches her and obviously helps her. We are pleased as this is Our aim. For all of you. To make you laugh out loud with realisation and epiphany as Lisa has done.

As We have said before, you are family to Us and We would do anything, as you would, to help family. We look down and see the torment and pain many of you experience and We are dispatched to assist you and to ensure your safe delivery.

There are many ways to get the messages from God across. Normal people such as yourselves receive the word of God through dreams sometimes and this helps them through trying times. Sometimes they write books about their experiences because it is too good to keep to themselves. We like this because it means it will reach as many people as possible. Where did these messages come from? Why Us of course. We Angels are the messengers of God. That is what We are here for. That is why We are speaking now. To familiarize you with Our language of love. The way We communicate can be through people but also through animals as Lisa is discovering whilst trying to write this chapter. She is trying to concentrate enough in order to hear Us whilst her cat is climbing all over the lap top.

We laugh because this little being who loves Lisa unconditionally is trying to get, yes you guessed it, love from her and she is getting frustrated. We then told her that this was a sign in and of itself. Always make time for love and never take it for granted. Especially when it's right in front of you in the form of your partner, your child and even your pet. No matter how insignificant the indicator is We urge you to make the most of it. For it is for your benefit that it is shown and if you miss it We don't want to hear you complain you don't have it. Animals are very potent sources of love and bring comfort to the elderly and the young. They are in touch with their God-source and love totally without condition. It is very sad to see them neglected or abused. They act as you should act and that is with total love and faith. We hope you do and We do not assume you don't love. However there are possibly times you feel disconnected and need to find your way home. We like that statement. 'Home'. We are your family and We want you to feel like We are 'home'. Which hopefully sends the message that you can turn to us any time.

We have spoken about innocence and how it is a pure expression of love. Both animals and children display this and We Angels are strongly around them close until they can care for themselves more. This does not mean We don't continue Our 'job' of caring for you as you get older. We laugh at your innocence in a loving way and then We feel nothing but love for you when you ask that We stay with you as you grow up. There is nothing more satisfying than staying by your side to see you graduate, to see you gain employment, to rejoice in your meeting and marrying your true love and then hanging around to see your children come into the world. We see God's creation in progress. And We smile when you lose your way. We smile because We know that all you have to do is call for Us. We know you can't stray far which is why We smile. Because We know and have faith that you will be fine.

Some of you talk to Us Angels and some talk directly to God. Either way is beneficial. Even when you talk to God it is Us Angels who usually intermediate. Not because God is too 'above' you to talk to you directly because He can do that if He wishes, but because it is Our role. We can come in close to you and whisper in your ear or stroke your energy field to impart wisdom and loving energy. You sometimes experience this as bright ideas and warm glow in your heart region. Sometime you get the 'warm fuzzie's no? For some reason all is right with the world and you feel like your body is relaxed and glowing. This indicates you are close to a state of being in your God-source. It also indicates We are close to you. We give you a brief glimpse of what it feels like to be 'tuned in' so you can do it for yourself. Only problem is you can sometimes not realise you can do it for yourself and freeze once it subsides thinking it only comes from an external force. We do it for you but one thing you don't understand is that We do it using what is already available within you. Bet you didn't know that! That means We work through you – literally! We come in close and use your energy field to create those sensations. This is something you most certainly can do for yourself. Lisa gave you an idea earlier how to sense us and to find the 'feeling' within you. Meditation is a good place to start. Don't worry We will be more than ready to answer once the channels have been established.

All you need to do is believe, as simple as that. We emphasise this strongly because you may just skip over the last sentence because it sounds like your run of the mill Angelic statement. But belief is so, so, so much the key. We can't stress it enough. Nobody needs to know if you're afraid of judgement. Our relationship with you is personal anyway and We feel it's not necessary to share it unless you are fully ready for it.

We are not afraid of being judged by others but We understand that you may feel judged and you can do what suits you. Many mainstream religions openly praise God and Us Angels and that is wonderful to us. They get so much comfort from communicating with us in this way and if this is how you wish to do it then so be it! We will work with you in whichever way you feel safe and comfortable. We by no means mean to make Our communication with you covert or suspiciously secret. We have nothing to hide and it is not in Our nature to do so as it would indicate fear and fear is not in Our vocabulary or nature. We ARE pure love. And for where love is there is no fear. Fear, as We are sure you have heard before, is a lack of love. This is not to say if you are fearful that you are unlovable or unloved. It means you have disconnected from it and can't see that the ability to reconnect is right under your nose. Like Lisa stepping around an Angel to get to the toilet. She was too focussed on the 'job' at hand to really SEE the Angel. She just stepped around the Angel oblivious to WHY the Angel was there. All she had to do was look up at the Angel's face to see what the message was. She wasn't tuned in at that particular moment and wasn't receptive. This is what it is like when you don't believe you can hear us. Well, almost. Lisa had some awareness but to see what the Angel wanted all she had to do was tune in.

This is what We want you to do.

It's just like tuning a radio. You strain to hear the familiar voice of your favourite disc jockey. You squint your eyes you put your ear closer to the radio and you listen intently. Then voila! You find it. This is a similar process you go through to listen to Us. We are laughing now at the thought of you, Our loved ones, squinting trying to listen. It's not literal, just a metaphor. We are encouraging intuitive perception. This could be seen as a precursor to developing psychic abilities but We are only wanting you to FEEL us and KNOW the Angelic energy so you can trust fully the messages that you receive. As Lisa has told you already, to further develop your intuitive skills then go to appropriate groups. We will be there with you.

Feeling Us is a multi-sensory experience and not just the figment of your imagination. You can hear Us and see Us and hopefully feel Us like tingles on your skin. Sometimes goose-bumps. But mainly it's just a 'knowing' and a warm glow which seems unflappable. We don't mess around and usually the first thing you get is the message you need to hear. Anything after that which may sound or feel uncertain then feel free to disregard the information. If you keep at Us We may not respond mainly because We don't pander to people or support unhealthy dependency. This does not mean We have left you and not work with you again. We just want you to realise that to go too far can be worse for you not better and that information you get after the initial contact can be misleading.

God created Us Angels to care for you and the world you live in. In His infinite wisdom He saw that you needed guidance and a friendly voice. He needed channels for pure divine love so that you can experience His love and protection through Us. We are an extension of His love. We are a family and you are an extension of that family. This is how We are integral to love's delivery.

When someone gets a message from Us they know We mean business and that it's genuine. We don't go in for frivolities. It essentially messed with your free will if We take it too far so We keep it brief and concise. To the point. We hear you laughing now. We know. Writing a book seems a bit long winded but there is a need and We offered to fulfil that need. We can carry a conversation just like you but when transmitting information or giving help to you We keep it business-like and cryptic. This book is a conversation with you via Lisa and We thoroughly enjoy having it. We use Lisa's point of reference and her sense of humour along with her vocabulary. This is what you call channelling. Lisa listens to Us and then translates it into wording that transmits understanding to you.

This is Our first written venture with Lisa and We hope for many more.

God's voice is spoken through Us and We then pass it on to you through several means. One is mentioned above. The other We have mentioned earlier and that is by direct contact with you with you either being aware of it or not.

Love is a universal language and is transmitted the same to everyone regardless of nationality. It is transmitted via the feeling sense and the person receiving it translates it into words that the majority can understand. Angelic presence is essential to transferring love. It's not that it's the only way. However it is more guaranteed to hit the mark. Nobody does it better! Even if We say so Ourselves.

Now to get back to why We are here. People listen to Angels and We are taken seriously. Your ancestors have documented past interactions with Us and there are many documented 'saints' whom are very cherished by God and Us. These beautiful souls did have important roles to play in your development as a peoples. They were engineered to be energetically more in touch with their God-source. They were practical and level headed and displayed a keen understanding of man's role on Earth and that you were to work your way back to God. You are God experiencing a physical incarnation in order to experience a new way of expressing love.

That is why We say you are a physical manifestation of God's love. Love being the currency of Angels and God.

God is in love with you and He wants you to be in love with him. We are in love with you and We are the messengers, the go betweens for you and God. We take pleasure in doing this. It is no problem at all and will continue for as long as God and you need us. We never have a dull moment and boy are We busy. It's all go for Us and We wouldn't have it any other way.

In your society if you mention to someone that you talk to God people will judge you. We don't judge you as We obviously know the truth. Yet if you talk to Angels it's slightly more acceptable. Yes it does sadden Us that this is so however We don't expect you to catch up until you are ready and after all you have free will and karma to deal with on Earth. So physical problems are a physical reality to you and just calling on Angelic help is not always socially acceptable. So peer pressure can suppress your desire to call on Us and God. No matter. We won't be offended just waiting for your return to the fold.

But for those people who are devout in whatever religion or belief system they belong to learn that prayer is a personal thing. They can pray more freely because in a church community it is the norm. Then there are those who are believers but who don't necessarily belong to a specific denomination. They may have spiritual beliefs that are not necessarily run of the mill 'normal' religions. They may even have what you term 'new age' beliefs. This is fine by Us too. We work along with what works best for you. Remember it is not Us Angels putting these restrictions on you but your fellow man. We never leave your side and watch and wait simply for you to turn to Us and say "Hello, I see you". There is no label on Us and We don't belong to one club and not the other.

We love to inspire you by Our very presence or the mention of Our names. For instance, We are talking through Gabriel who then talks through Lisa. Or rather Gabriel talks through Lisa on the collective's behalf. Lisa is working hard to not taint the information with her own thoughts and We appreciate this greatly. It is not easy to do but she is experiencing another new level of trust and sometimes We have to assure her that what she has just written for Us is going to work and not make a fool of her. So she sighs and gets on with it. This is a challenge for anyone who We work through in this way. To hand over to Us and just allow whatever comes through to come through. To not question what is said to them or interfere with the way it's related or the exact wording that is used. For the word of God has to be passed on somehow. And that is what we are doing. It is a pleasure to work through ordinary, everyday people who are usually down to Earth and gentle. This way We can be sure of a message being conveyed in a non-offensive way and with love.

Love is a powerful force. It conquers and surmounts huge obstacles. It buoys you through major difficulties.

Like We mentioned before it is a language with which Angels talk to you. Whether it be via the spoken or written word or just sensations and visual images. As long as you are open to possibilities you can choose the way you want to communicate. Usually prayer is sufficient but in some cases which can be extreme. We do show Ourselves in order to show absolute support. Miracles can be delivered by Us and important information can be conveyed. Major milestones such as the birth of Jesus have been announced by Us and they have been noted in your history books.

When you see someone praying it is them connecting with God and Us. They are having a private moment and you need to respect that. Of which We are sure you will. You may not be able to see Angels standing around them but rest assured We are and listening intently. When in this state the slightest sign is accepted with no questions asked. A sign might be a familiar smell or a brush on the cheek or a visual flash of what to do. This is very private and personal. It is also specific to that person's point of reference. Only they know what We said to them and that is how it should be. We want a relationship with you and this is how We do it. Be gentle with yourselves and allow Us to help you and heal you if you need it.

You truly are God's children and will be cherished and protected as such. Even in the most extreme circumstances We are present. We know your faith is truly tested in these circumstances yet We cannot step in always because it is what you chose to experience.

We are present at your birth and we are present at your passing. Along with your guides and deceased loved ones. We can help guide people to the light and We escort them into their next life. We make no decisions for them nor do We interfere with that process. We simply support and encourage. It is all done in the name of love. Mutual love and admiration. We admire your courage in choosing an Earthly life. It can be a blissful life or a harsh one. Trust Us you've experienced all types of existences and lifetimes. It's like changing hats as one of your sayings goes.

By reading a book like this one you will hopefully be uplifted and inspired. You will probably be influenced to come down to Earth by life's events and be as you were before but maybe you can re-read this book at times of need. That is one of the purposes of this project and We hope you will take Us up on it.

Credibility is one thing We could be aiming for. But We know better. We know that We do not need to prove Our existence and the people who read this will not need it either. It is a written dialogue between you and Us which works on a subtle level. This will weed out the people who are not serious or really committed to strengthening their link to God and Us this way.

You have choice and if this book doesn't do it for you then just calmly put it down or better yet pass it on to someone who will make good use of it. We are not going to diminish because of it and it obviously wasn't the right time to connect with those readers. Don't worry, they'll catch up.

Once you've accepted that We Angels exist then that's half the problem solved. Don't leave it until the last minute and then get angry because We don't suddenly manifest in front of you. It doesn't work like that.

You need to develop a relationship with Us which includes having total faith in Us and Our existence. Then prayer and dialogue. Then, and this is the biggy, LISTEN to Us. Try to pretend you can hear Us and act 'as if' you have received something from Us. The first thing that comes to mind is usually our response. Don't dismiss it right away. If you keep trying after that with the same question and you start getting muddled answers you then need to stop and take a break. Come back to it when you're ready. We aren't going anywhere and already know what you're going to ask as well as knowing the answer before you say it. We just wait for your signal.

No matter what you do or where you go We will be there for you and nothing will make us turn away. Not even if you commit a horrible crime. We don't condone that behaviour, however you are still a child of God and at heart We know that deep down you are still capable of great love. What you've done on the surface, in the physical, is not the whole you and the part that is still from the God-source is still just that. What is here on Earth, in the physical, is just the tip of the iceberg and you are so much more. You will face the karma you've incurred on the physical and We will be there to help you through it but will not stop it from happening.

Whatever you may have done will have to be dealt with on the physical. But the essence of who you are in God's eyes is still loved. Like We said, We DO NOT condone heinous crimes done on the physical but the spirit of those who have done such things is still loved. You are not to know what has happened to them to get them to that point and they will have to pay the price but they know this and it is part of their growth.

We cannot and do not judge as all need Our help. We have to be unconditional. We do it for you and the innocents. For if these criminals are healed by Us then they are not likely to repeat the acts. We are 'integral' to their healing and connection to God so that they can see the error of their ways. Wish them love not hate. Not because you are gullible but because at this very moment you are stronger than they are. Forgive them not just for their sake but for yours and your loved ones sake. For if you hang on to anger it will cause you to implode. You can't move on to bigger and better things if you're looking back with hate and anger. It causes tension and stress in your body and in the end you are the one who's suffering. It is better to release in order to step forward into more rewarding and fulfilling experiences and feelings. Why hinder yourself by holding on. Lean on Us and allow Us to take the load for you. Just ask. Don't be shy. We just need to be asked first.

You are probably not used to communicating with Us and may not be aware just how much We can do for you. We are the 'action team' through which God works through to help you. This is how We are integral to LOVE's delivery.

"What we can do to nurture love. How to make sure there's an abundance as opposed to lack"

Love comes from the God-source when you look at it from a macrocosm point of view. But in the microcosm it manifests in you on an individual level. We Angels are the 'go betweens' between these two states of being.

In God's existence Love is all that there is and it permeates through everything He touches. All you have to do is let Him touch your heart.

Love is a wonderful experience and is almost addictive. Although true love is not that at all for that would indicate impropriety. Real love is not dysfunctional or controlling and it should be fluid and free. It should move through you and not be caught and trapped just like a butterfly and held too close in a suffocating way.

It is a precious commodity and you should treat it with reverence. It is also seemingly not easy to come by and that when you do get it to treasure it and nurture it.

It is actually not that hard to obtain of course, but it does depend on your perception. Once discovered it can be hard to switch off. This can be a good thing and also not so good. We by no means wish to condemn someone for loving this way. We just wish to show you that if you take it to extremes it can be not how it is intended. God's love is intended to uplift, protect, inspire and comfort not control and limit.

We can only guide you to how you are meant to express love. Let Us emphasise that We do not condemn you if your love for another becomes dysfunctional nor are We trying to make you out to be bad or unacceptable.

You are still loved deeply by Us and that is enough for Us to be honest enough with you to tell you the truth. This is because We want you to experience it in the way that is best for you and how it is intended to be experienced. Outside of these guidelines it becomes something other than true, pure love. It can be known as co-dependency, lust or possessiveness. This is just an imbalance and what you may not realise is that love can be reinstated. It's never too late to return to the fold. We will take you back no questions asked.

Some of you think you've lost touch with love and the God-source. We use Lisa as an example again (trust Us she fights with Us about Us using her). She is starting to struggle with doubt about what she thinks is her writing and all that it's about. It is of course Us working through her. She bemoans to Us that she doesn't think there is any more information in her to give. This is showing her brief disconnection from her source of love. And her God-source. We have not left her and are still raring to go but she is convinced it is her writing this so she thinks she'll run dry. Then We laugh in love as she sits down and connects and voila it flows again! Where does it come from? Us of course and from the source of all love – God. She forgets that We will never 'run dry'. She forgets that it's Us who are supplying the information not her. It is a big trust issue for her. Not that she doesn't trust Us but that she isn't good enough.

Sometimes love is hard to shake. Just like when you separate from a partner. It takes time to heal from a break up and love cannot simply dissipate over-night. Because love is a precious commodity you may misunderstand and hang onto it thinking it is too precious to lose. So the object of your love is your focus and this leads to pain on your part as this ex-love of yours moves on into another relationship. Love is experienced phenomenologically to each and every one of you. Each person experiences it typical to themselves and their conditioning. According to their point of reference they will see love how they've been taught to. By their parents and siblings and their friends.

Those who cling to it have learnt to base their love on fear. Fear of loss or deprivation. Technically this is not true love.

We again are talking of love as an energy form. This kind of 'love' feels and in a way acts like love but is not thoroughly love in its truest form. True love is not possessive or controlling or demanding. It does not exist where fear is because fear is another energy form. Another currency. We most certainly don't poo poo those who may be in the fear based zone. We love them dearly and these stray lambs are the ones We Angels have to herd back to the main flock. We have faith in you and know that it is just a temporary jaunt off into an emotional testing ground that forges the mettle in you.

You cannot stray far for We are with you always and are only a breath away. We see the glints of colour in your hair, the jewellery in your ears the smell of your perfume and the colour of your clothes. We are that close to you.

And sometimes you see, sense and smell Us around you too. You may see a shape in the form of Us Angels or lights or even smell the smell of roses which is a common scent indicating Our presence.

Just experiencing this can convert even the shrewdest of cynics sometimes. Seeing and feeling Us around can be life changing and for the better. The energy exchange of just knowing we are around is an exchange with Us. A deal if you will. That if you truly believe in Us then We shall make Our presence felt. We Angels like to have a little fun too. We like it sometimes when you do this because it is how you learn to transfer the energy source which is love. Your necessary testing of Us (not the defiant and obstinate testing) is like a toddler testing a parent to see how much they love them because it feels good and when that parent does show them it reinforces the love. This may sound disrespectful towards Us Angels but don't worry, We know how to look after Ourselves and We know when it's inappropriate. We allow it to occur because when the realisation finally comes it'll sink in better and then there will be no struggle to believe. It'll prove itself through you FEELING it.

To feel it means you have got the gist of how to tap into it and that is what We aim for. You'll then realise that it isn't that hard. It can be sensed as that warm loving feeling just like a warm hug from your lover. You have a moment where everything seems clear and your senses are heightened. You feel like you can just lean back into the arms of your invisible helper. It's hard though isn't it? To let go and trust you'll be caught. You are so used to being in control and aware. It doesn't dull your sensibilities to actually let go. You can still be acutely aware and alert. Just be so along with Us.

Human conditioning is a tough nut to crack. The attitude of 'prove it' makes it hard for people to let go and allow themselves to be absorbed into the Angelic way of seeing and being and not to forget loving.

You all need evidence and that is not something We Angels will submit to as if We owe it to you. However those humble souls who approach us with reverence and kindness will receive such in return. No questions asked. We are no fools Ourselves and can see right through any charade. We read you so well and know how genuine you are. It isn't very hard to see. We see it in your energy fields and auras.

Your body language and verbal skills too. All of you play a part in how you approach Us and interact with Us.

We talk of this because We Angels are integral to transmitting God's love to you and We know you on a personal level. Enough to want to help you experience love in its purest form.

Its almost akin to an engine in your car. You have a battery (a source of energy eg. love) and you have the engine (you) however you need the connector wires to get the energy or power from the battery to the engine. You need a way of transferring enough energy to sustain a smoothly purring engine. Add some connector wires and voila! You have lift off. The connector wires represent your connectedness to God and Us.

Another analogy is that experiment where two tomato plants are grown. One with no attention given to it other than watering. The other is given undivided attention such as gentle strokes and softly spoken encouragements and even classical music. The experiment is to show that a living entity thrives better with loving energy given to it at regular intervals. Lo and behold it works. The plant which receives loving attention appears to thrive and grows remarkably taller and fuller than the other. This can apply to man too. Some children in orphanages or in third world countries have what is known as failure to thrive. This is because they are without the love of a parent or loved one usually because they've lost them to illness and death. There is not enough loving energy given to them and they then have stunted growth and psycho-emotional issues.

Our hearts break for these beautiful little ones. We offer as much help as We can and try to lead new loved ones to them who will love them as they deserve.

As you can see it is important that living sentient beings need love in order to exist. Just as you need food and water. It gives you sustenance and energy to live your lives fully as God intended.

Love is the fuel upon which man survives. He can survive without it but thrives much better with it. If a person receives enough love then they are enabled enough to give love. For if they were bereft of a loving source then they would be a lot like a dry well. Not that they aren't good, kind people, but that it would be difficult to come out of their comfort zone long enough to give and receive love. It would be alien to them what it would be like to be loved. Or at least they may have forgotten. Like We said before, it's never too late to pick up where you left off. If you've experienced this type of lack then turn your face to the sun. Let it warm you with it's glow. This is how you can find your way back to the love of God.

You are not being punished by having lack of love as you are as deserving as anyone else. You can be bitter about it or you can turn it into a positive. You choose. Either way you will still be loved by Us. We are pleased when you choose to turn it around and this means you are more connected than you probably first thought. For to turn it around into a positive is an act of self-love. Surprise surprise.

It's a lesson in self-love to accept yourself as you are and not so much as how others see you. You need to find sustenance from within not always from outside.

Nobody can deny love given to you by a dear family member, child or partner is as sweet as you can get, but essentially you need to be prepared to love yourself equally as much. It creates the foundation from which stability arises. You have to see that you are worthy of love and not just from those around you, but from yourself. If you have children you will have an idea of how important it is to show your children how to express love to others. But you'll be doing them a big service by showing them how to love themselves. You can start by leading by example. Yes it's a wonderful feeling to have that love given to you. It makes you feel glorious and invincible. But let's face it, when it subsides you can't draw on external sources of love. It happens, people fall out of love or the love changes. If you have a good sense of yourself and self-worth then maintaining it even after a separation can be easier and you will have that to draw on. As that saying goes, building your home on a solid foundation will ensure that it will withstand the elements. Just knowing that you were loved dearly once means you are worthy of love. New love is bound to come your way again.

If you are in an abusive or loveless relationship and feel like you've never known love We definitely want to help. Your definition of where love comes from might be limiting your options for you. This is why people don't always realise they can turn to Us. Because We, to some, are an unknown quantity. It's not physical and in front of you so it can't exist you may think. You don't think to turn to Us as We are not visible. Just think what you're missing out on. We adore you and long for you to return the feelings. You are only limited by your faith or lack thereof. Imagine We are behind you. Imagine We have put Our arms around you. Feel the warmth from Our bodies and feel Our energy. It should feel blissful and content. Also it should feel unconditional and all encompassing. You feel relaxed and safe. Another way you can experience Us is how Lisa seems to and that is joy and laughter. Her face lights up and she chortles away. It can be discerning to those she is reading for but she reassures them it is just the absolute bliss of basking in God's and the Angel's energy and glory.

It doesn't demean or belittle the seriousness of your worries and troubles but is meant to be infectious and healing (how's that for an angelic oxymoron?). To be healed by basking in the joy provided by God and the Angels. Laughter, after all, is the greatest healer. Remember as a child how you were cajoled into re-joining the frivolities of a family party after having a fall out with your brother or sister? It was a serious aberration on their part and you are determined not to forgive but whilst you are staging this walkout and strike you are missing out on all the fun. Then that favourite uncle surfaces again, you know the one who tickles you and 'gets' you. He tickles you and teases you, daring you to show them what for. Eventually he makes you giggle and then it doesn't seem so hard to forgive for having fun is far more important than sulking.

This leads Us to discuss the act of forgiveness. This is such an important thing for you to do. In itself it is an expression of love. For when you love enough it will make it easier to forgive. To forgive someone means you have enough self-love and worth that you don't want to cause any more stress or pain to yourself nor the other party. This act comes from a place of security. People who can do this are secure in themselves. By people We mean everybody. Everyone has the capacity to forgive yet finding it is an issue in itself. Getting your head around the possibility of actually forgiving your enemy can be tricky. That is where it starts though and you need to put everything in perspective. Don't allow anger and frustration to seethe within you even if the other party were to blame. The more you allow this to happen the more it will push love out of reach. It displaces it and pushes it out of reach just like the cuckoo chick pushes the others out of the nest.

How else are you going to move forward in your life if you don't forgive and release old grudges?

Love your enemy despite what they have done. We say this for your benefit more than anything. Not to love them in a vulnerable and pathetic way but in a strong way. Coming from a place of inner strength. The core of you which is unflappable. Where you are routed to the ground and know yourself so well that you are willing to stand up for your rights. If you do so then don't forget to forgive. As you won't be able to move onto the next phase in your life. You won't feel complete if you don't. Forgive them despite what they've done. Your anger and hate will be a waste of energy. It drags you down and into a living hell.

Why go there? You also may not know all the details of your enemy's life and influences. They have their point of view and it may be valid to them. But you can only concentrate on YOU and the only way to ease your inner turmoil may be to release grudges and anger.

Love can't cohabitate with hate and anger. It's one or the other. It is wise to opt for forgiveness because it frees you.

To do this you are working towards an abundance as opposed to lack of love. God doesn't like to see his children fight. He also doesn't want you to perpetuate the energy of unforgiveness as this contaminates others around you. Especially your children.

Forgiving yourself is very important. You may associate forgiveness with others and not yourself. If you can't forgive yourself then how can you forgive others? Those who have trouble releasing toxic feelings for other people usually are transferring pain from previous events. They think that what has just happened as traumatic but it feels as such due to already existing, unresolved pain. This could be known as transference and projection. If you forgive yourself you will be doing yourself a favour for future life events. It's because you don't release and forgive that causes pain to accumulate within you to come out later on when a new problem arises. Already existing pain compounds any newly acquired pain. This wouldn't happen if you learnt to forgive and release. Again it is an energy exchange. If you have static electricity built up because of your synthetic clothing you need to release it and when you do so it crackles and hurts a little in your knuckles. This is similar to releasing and forgiving. Sure it hurts a little (which is a deterrent) but you need to do it to release the charge or you'll affect another when you touch them. We can hear you laughing about Us comparing forgiveness with static electricity. What a bright spark you are. Truly and honestly We say to you that to forgive is not just an act of kindness to the other party it's also to yourself. To forgive frees you up fully to be able to love.

It affects you physically and can cause tension and tension headaches. Aches and pains such as arthritis. Throat issues also.

We Angels try to heal you on many levels to help you release past hurts. This is why tuning in to Us will help you no end. Have a conversation with Us as this is a bit like self-counselling. Except We are actually listening. This brings Us to prayer. Prayer is a way for you to talk to God and Us Angels when you're in need of an ear to listen. Prayer, in your society, is more acceptable than being seen as talking to 'thin air' which is actually you talking to Us. You can listen and talk to Us out loud in the privacy of your own home or you can 'think' your communication. Prayer is more acceptable in places like churches or temples. Prayer doesn't have to be audible on the physical and you can be sitting on the bus on the way to work and close your eyes and tune in to Us to pray silently. Prayer is a personal thing. It doesn't matter how you pray if you do it out loud or in your head. What is important is that you feel like your load is shared. That you are supported and loved. This is what We mean by developing a relationship with Us. It is no different than a physical, human relationship. Just that We have a slightly different form than you and a different way of existing. This however should not be a hindrance to you finding and talking to Us. All that restricts you is your belief systems. You believe that We need to be physically in front of you or that if you talk to Us others will judge you as being loopy. Just be prudent as to how you go about it. We don't want you to be secretive and We do want you to be proud to be associated with Us but discretion may be needed as to appropriate time and place. Mainly so the quality of our and your communication will be maintained. Not because We are afraid to have you acknowledge Us. We just want the best for you. Let's face it your connection to God and Us is important and worthy of personal uninterrupted attention.

To develop your relationship with Us means you are taking steps toward loving yourself more thoroughly. You are taking the time to invest positive energy into your unseen support team. (Lisa is giggling and is picturing Us in team colours like your football teams) People see Us Angels as not having senses of humour and being very serious. Sorry but that is not altogether true. Yes We have a serious job to do and We take it extremely seriously. But our sense of humour is more subtle than yours and so it can be mistakenly thought We are humourless. We have a serenity about Us and so We actually 'get' your humour but just experience it as blissful joy internally and not necessarily as loud raucous laughter. How can We NOT have a sense of humour? Your laughter is an expression of joy which translates into love. We ARE love and so experience the joy you do. We highly recommend laughter and those who are genuinely jolly people are so happy because they accept themselves and let go of self-consciousness. They love themselves enough to laugh freely and without fear of judgement and if there was criticism they would be able to confidently respond to it. This is how We want you all to be. We know some of you have difficulty with being openly yourselves but don't worry We will arrange for you to improve your skills in this department. We are not saying you are deficient now as you are perfect in Our eyes. You just have to realise that things don't have to be the way you think. You sometimes perceive that there is a lack in love and acceptance and because of this you hold yourself in and dim your light. We want to see you put yourself out there and dare to be different. Viva les difference! It's okay to have a template to work from like organised religion, but it is truly marvellous when you bend the rules and be an individual. It means you are living life how you were meant to and that is in a creative way. If you copy everyone else you are repeating the mistakes that they make and you end up going in circles. God is in a constant flux of creation and it demonstrates when YOU do this that you are growing because of what you learn. Otherwise you will be in a state of 'stuckness'. Life is your learning ground and you need to really experience life not sit it out like you are on a bus which someone else is driving.

Have faith in you. We do. Have faith that you're capable and have value. If you have this everything will slip into place like it's meant to. To value yourself is to love yourself and to love yourself means you can love others unconditionally and in a healthy way. You may fluctuate in and out of control of this until you get used to it. Nobody will condemn you for lapsing.

When you find that love within you it will get easier to find the feeling of abundance. Because when you're content due to having love, then you appreciate what you already have. There are some who overlook what positives are in their lives and bemoan that they have nothing. What they are saying is that they don't feel loved and so lack abundance. Of course in many occasions this is the case. But they always have the opportunity to turn it around. We are not being insensitive to those who truly suffer. Our love goes out to them and We will support them as much as they'll let Us. We are trying to show you that despite the hardships you endure sometimes the only way to deal with it is to move forward and utilise the love sent from God. As you say, 'Things can only get better from here'.

We may sound a little flippant but actually We are intending to sound optimistic and positive. We understand that sometimes you feel like you've hit rock bottom and that it seems insurmountable. But we're sure the last thing you want is miserable Angels moaning about the work load God has got them doing. We know that to get out of any situation regardless of how dire, you really need Us to be helpful and positive not the other way around. The last thing We want is to be counter-productive to your cause.

To nurture love within you you have to first recognise that you have it. We can see it from here. How beautiful a sight it is to behold. Of course you have it in you. You are of God and He IS love so what does that make you?

We may repeat ourselves sometimes but We are going to until you get it.

We know you are capable of anything you put your mind to and that includes finding the love you feel bereft of. It is no laughing matter when one of God's children is abused and attacked and have their security threatened. Even tortured and harmed or raped. There is no way We condone these actions and believe Us when We say those who do this will be dealt with in the appropriate way. They have lessons to learn also such as compassion, which, as you know, is an aspect of love.

No matter how badly you were treated there comes a time where you have to pick yourself up and dust yourself down and get on with things. You're not expected to jump right to it and your suffering needs honouring and validating. We want you to leave behind the past and create a new future. Believe Us when We say We know how much you have suffered. And you may say that its impossible to get back to where you were before the damage was done. We do not take this lightly. It is important though that you realise that the only way is up and that the sooner you start the journey to claw your way back to normality the sooner you can let your love shine again. And We can resume Our relationship with you.

If you work on the things We have discussed here then We expect love to come back into your life or be enhanced if you already have it. We were discussing hardships in order to help you burn off the dross and to release any programming that is still damaging to you. Even if the cause of the programming is because of someone else. There may a part of you that is angry and defiant about releasing someone else's damaging actions toward you. But We say that even if these people were to be hung drawn and quartered you still have to work through the pain. You would still be where you are when you need to be somewhere else in order to feel again. Of course you're not expected to do it all on your own and that is why We keep reminding you that We are here and to call on Us. You are probably used to being self-reliant and have your feet in the 'real' world. But who's to say Our world is any less 'real'. If you haven't experienced it then you haven't tried hard enough. Half-hearted attempts won't get you very far. In for a penny in for a pound as Lisa would say (I wish they'd stop quoting me. I'm embarrassed now: Lisa).

We had this issue with Lisa but thankfully she gets it now.

You may slip sometimes and feel like it's one step forward one step back but tenacity and persistence are qualities We are trying to help you exercise. Just like a muscle.

Once you find your way home to God with Our help then you can feel love once more and then you can accept abundance. All of the above is driven towards you nurturing yourself instead of punishing. And if you nurture yourself enough you will feel secure enough to realise abundance.

You will have abundance when you understand that you and only you create it and stubbornly refusing to believe it comes from you then you will stay there. In limbo. Our hands are tied when you do this and are itching to help but can't because of your free will. Yes you have free will and no-one can interfere. Not even Us Angels. How you handle this predicament is your responsibility and We can only guide and reassure. Please think about asking Us for help for We can assist you when you ask. Remember We work in a subtle way and the help We offer will be in a non-dramatic way. We can heal your hurt by whispering reassuring words and guiding things to go your way without influencing another's free will. We can help by way of aligning synchronistic events which will allow you to recognise lessons and give you a chance to correct your trajectory. It's Our way of giving you a clue like in a game of charades. Ultimately you are the creator in your life and We are your support team. Once you realise your potential We hope nothing will stop you from rising to be the best you can possibly be. Then you will have abundance. When you know you have everything that you need and want then you will know you have abundance. To have abundance does not relate to your material wealth, although that can help. Especially if you've had little throughout your life. But abundance is a knowing. A knowing that you are well looked after and provided for by God and the Angels. It also indicates you can look after yourself and you are free from limiting thoughts and belief patterns. That you are managing your conditioning and allowing yourself to feel like you can manifest what you desire. Abundance is a state of mind and being. So BE it. THINK it. KNOW it.

"Those who are sent to show love"

There are moments where you may wonder what love is supposed to look like. And what it feels like. Do you catch it like you catch the flu? (That's Angelic humour for you: Lisa) Do you buy it at the supermarket?

Love is very precious and needs to be cherished not taken for granted. Those who don't sense love around them are not tuned in or receptive. They think it should come to them no questions asked. Of course it is all around them and ready to be tapped into but to expect it in this way will simply be like waiting for a bus on the wrong street corner and expecting the bus to find you. You need to look for it and be receptive to it. You need to be less aloof and stubborn. Standing on that corner expecting the bus to change its route just to accommodate you is being inflexible and stubborn. Love is not conditional but it does need SOME input from you. You can go in search of the bus stop that is right for you. And then sit back, relax and be receptive. Remember it's a relationship God wants to have with you so there's a little give and take involved. 'God helps those who help themselves'.

Sometimes there are certain people who seem sent from God. They have a role and that is to demonstrate love and how to give it and receive it. They show love in all its guises. These people are in tune with their higher selves and are more centred and grounded. This makes being in touch with the higher realms easier and safer. Mostly these loved ones are happy leading lives of modesty. They are usually down to Earth, easy going, level headed and gentle beings. They have no need for frivolities and will usually say so. That is not a priority for them. Helping mankind is.

Love is a priority and living the word of God. These people are in constant contact with Us Angels and know that We do actually exist. They know how to contact Us and how to use Us to help. Because of this they make good teachers and leaders. The most obvious person like this is Jesus. He is the most loved and well known messenger of God. The son of God. Where would you be today without him? He leads many a person into the arms of God through his love and devotion to God and to you.

Nearly everyone has heard of Jesus and his disciples and the lessons he taught. Regardless of which denomination you belong to Jesus is held in such high regard and with reverence. His life was a lesson taught by him leading by example. He showed you that the ultimate sacrifice was one of pure love and faith. He wanted to show you how to really live and how to really love. And that to show complete faith in God by sacrificing what is most precious. Sacrificing your life. Not necessarily to death but to give life itself over to God. Taking the life you have been given and living it to its fullest. That is what God wants of you. To take life by the horns and really live it in God's name.

Buddha is another example and the belief system that is Buddhism is a wonderful one and We Angels respect it for what it stands for.

There are people who have been canonized as saints and they lived real lives not that long ago. Some led lives of piety and abstinence such as those who joined the clergy and became nuns or priests.

Padre Pio was made a saint and is famous for his healing abilities. He had a church and a hospital and lived in service to heal and help those in true need.

Then there's St. Mother Teresa who became a nun and eventually heard a calling to live and assist the poorest people in Calcutta in India.

These people lived in relatively modern times and yet chose to live humble lives in service to God.

When they were alive they were living examples of how to exist in pure love. They enacted God's love and were love incarnate. For what greater gesture of love that sacrificing your life to the service of God with others welfare as your goal?

God does not expect you all to go out and give everything up. Your children need a roof over their heads after all and that is a noble profession in itself. Being a parent. You try your best to live life 'right' to show your little ones how to live and love. You try to guide them on the straight and narrow and you do your best to teach them how to express and feel love and kindness. This is an extremely important job and by no means do We urge you to jeopardise that. For you may be shaping future Saints or pillars of your community. Now isn't that a thought? Your child may have an important job sometime in the future. That may be just that they become a corporate leader who is also known as a generous boss and supporter of charities. They may become well known and use their fame to promote worthy causes. But then again they may be just an ordinary Joe Bloggs who decides to become a doctor and finds a calling to work with underprivileged or in third world countries. What-ever they do as long as they are kind to one another and respectful of God then you can consider yourself as doing a great job. For this is all We ask of you. It's not always your or your children's calling to be living saints but We hope that you and they will be influenced by what this type of person represents. Love!

After all you all need it don't you? It's what keeps you alive. Without it you would not thrive. For those who have not got love on the physical plane then just reach out to Us Angels. Even though you can't always see Us doesn't mean We aren't there. You may think that that isn't enough to satisfy your hunger for love, but that is being closed minded. Be open to the possibility that We are there and are ready, willing and able to enfold you with Our wings.

To deny this is to deny yourself of love which does exist. You'll never know unless you try it. Try to tap into the divine energy and allow it to wash over you. Imagine it is happening. Humour Us again. Imagining it is happening is how you go about it and if you do it often enough with enough trust that you'll get something then you'll build up a good connection. When you feel a warm glow your initial reaction might be to dismiss it as your imagination. Well it IS your imagination as that is through which We work. In using your imagination We are not using something that is fictional. It's a very real dimension that you're tapping into and here We can liaise with each other there. But if this does not appeal to you then We understand fully. There are other ways to communicate with Us and to ask for Our help. Prayer in spoken or written form is effective.

We need people like Mother Teresa to show Us unconditional love and devotion to God. It may seem extreme but by her living as she did she was making a statement. That it is possible to live and be wealthy without material possessions. Also to demonstrate that love is all that is needed as nourishment for the soul. Compassion is another reason and as We discussed earlier is another expression of love. Mother Teresa and all the other Saints were living examples of compassion and sacrifice. They lived a life totally dedicated to God and living as man was intended, as loving compassionate and humble souls. Their aim was to put others before them and this is as God wanted it. To be generous with your love and time and sometimes, just sometimes being a Good Samaritan. We urge you to learn from these examples in order to let go of the material world. To live wholly in the light of God and be kind to one another.

To have total faith and trust in God's plan for you. He won't give you anything you can't cope with. You are special to him and knows that you may have lost your way. That is the purpose of having spiritual motivators such as Jesus in your life. He lived as he was meant to and had total unconditional regard for all mankind and held no anger at his oppressor. He accepted what his role was and lived it fully and with love. There was a reason why Jesus was born and that was to live as an example to mankind that you don't have to live in fear as this cuts you off from your God-source. He was truly connected to God and was unswerving in his loyalty.

What you don't realise is that you don't really need others to show you the way as you have all that you need within you and all you have to do is tap into this resource which is God-source. But these people were sent to show you your abilities and capacity. They are not different from you or separate from you. They are just like you. They had a calling though to live as you should live and love how you should love. We are not implying you are unable to love or are incompetent. We are just illustrating how you can love more fully. And sometimes it's more effective to illustrate by example. These people were willing participants.

They had a job to do and they did so whole heartedly. They knew that man had lost his way and needed lighthouses to light the way. We all come from God and if that is the case you should understand that you are more than able to find him within this incarnation.

Lighthouses is a term that Lisa likes to use. She uses it when she refers to the mentors she has had in her life. Mentors is very apt. People like Mother Teresa are mentors. As are the local heroes like doctors, nurses, firemen (who risk their very lives to save others) and teachers. Those who devote their time to helping others and sometimes at their own expense. You need mentors to break the ice and try innovative ways of helping others. To lead the way for those who are lost and alone. They are taking up the mantle of leadership and education. What better way to get across God's message. To impart information that helps those around them to learn that the only way to be is to love and allow love into their lives. As you can see the main theme of this book is LOVE and it is important that We Angels illustrate it in many different ways so that it gets the message home. To get you to understand that it's only as easy as thinking and believing you can achieve love. You may already have love in your life but We are talking about the divine love you get from a relationship with God. This can fulfil you and strengthen the other loves of your life not detract from them or make them insignificant. Having God and the Angels in your life should only strengthen your love for others in your life. It should give you the motivation to love more thoroughly. Knowing that you have Us on side should strengthen your resolve and commitment to living in the light of God for doing so will make life a lot easier to live. It can enhance your life and relationships. You can conquer most anything if you are aware you have God on your side.

You have spiritual leaders among you now who live to just spread the message of love. They are ground-breakers in their own right and are non-conformists. They allow for diversity in belief systems but still work closely with God's word.

It's not that We don't have faith in you because We do. Sometimes it's more effective having physical representatives on Earth who can speak for Us. Especially for those who find it hard to imagine what We're like and not sure if they can feel Us around. They can, they just don't realise. Or try. How can they when society tends to force people to suppress these urges and ridicules them for using their intuition.

To have another human to demonstrate and teach ways of loving and caring can be healing to some. They relay how to experience it and how to find it internally as well as externally. Some of Our children require this guidance and in receiving it are healed internally. That is a joy to Us to see Our loved ones finding peace and harmony from this healing communication. It's the energy exchange of love again! You plug yourself into the God-source and presto, you feel better as God's love is downloaded into your energy field. Lisa likens it to the internet. We don't dislike this analogy although it's not quite what We had in mind. The internet is impersonal and not warm and heartfelt as communication with Us is. You can actually feel Us (if you try) and We can heal you. We ask you, can a computer do this? (Yet another Angelic joke: Lisa)

Now a real, live, in the flesh teacher who can pass on God's word really is worth his/her weight in gold. Bless them for they have dedicated their lives to sharing the joy they have found in God.

Bless you for being you. We love you.

"How to feel what love feels like"

Ah. Now this is a tough one. Why? Because it's a personal experience. It is unique to every single one of you.

We can only present a model of what love is.

Love, as We have said before, is an energy. It runs through all of you and has its origins in God. God creates from love and He created you. Realisation of your full potential is just behind the veil. All you have to do is pull it aside briefly to get a glimpse.

Being in touch with one's creator means you are close to feeling what true love is.

You know if you're in touch with love when you feel joyful and blissful. You feel strong and unflappable in your resolve. You feel supported and cherished. You glow from the inside and have a big smile on your face.

You don't need to have physical proof of love as God can provide this love. For those of you who have little by way of physical love We want you to know that there is another source of love other than a physical one. We don't want you to go without it and are suggesting another way of obtaining it. And it's FREE!

You are the source of love. You probably don't realise it yet. That you are all that you need. Yet society has us believing that it has to come from an external source and that you have to work hard to get it. Of course you have to make an effort but having love is effortless. And living in love makes other things effortless. Because when you are in touch with that love you can take on anything.

Those who feel bereft of love and that things are hopeless may think that this kind of thinking is 'away with the fairies'.

We haven't glossed over it as if your deficiency in love doesn't exist. If you don't 'get' what We are saying you are not listening closely enough. Love is an energy which can be tapped into like when you plug a heater into the wall socket. Its source is probably one that you don't recognise because you expect love to be more on the physical. If it is not demonstrated on the physical then it can't exist in any other way. Wrong. Be open to alien ways of feeling love. We say 'alien' even though We know it isn't. It's a spiritual form of love which many already know exists and it exists like a currant that runs through each and every one of you. This is why We refer to it as an energy form. Like electricity. You can tap into it and feel it. It is real, even more real than the physical manifestation. Real because it's constant and unconditional. It is not monitored and meted out in accordance with rules or expectations. It is completely free and available to all. We don't want to play games with you or lead you astray. We are genuine in Our intent and work hard towards your education of where love actually comes from. We know you are intelligent people and We do not wish to detract from that by sounding patronising. But you are God's children. A term of endearment. One that indicates a role of learning and experiencing. That is why you have been born, to experience a physical life and all that goes with it. Including physical and spiritual love in all it's guises.

The spiritual love may seem like its illusive and that you have to run around it to find it. But if you centre yourself and listen to your inner voice, the kind voice that supports you and motivates you, you will find that love actually comes from within yourself. Even the love you have from a loved one comes from within. 'How so?' We hear you say. Well you see the love in the eyes of your child or lover and then turn inwards to find what it evokes in you. It evokes a warm cared for feeling. So are these people sending you love or are you just perceiving it? We say both. It is encoding and decoding. One is where you construct the message to send (eg. The message of love) the other the receiving of the message and reconstructing it inside your head and heart. Intuitively you can feel it too. Like a glow internally and you can feel the energy exchange between you and your loved one. When you hug you feel, intuitively, the love transference between you and your loved one. That is the point of the hug. You are sentient beings and you can actually FEEL love in a hug. When a person's aura merges with another's it makes you feel a glow surround you. This aura is your energy field through which you transmit love to another in a sensory way. You can sense this aura when you stand next to someone and you can feel the warmth emanating off their body. There's a definite edge to their aura and you feel this even though you aren't physically touching.

Sometimes people hug you and it feels cold or it just doesn't register in a warm way despite their best intentions. It doesn't mean they don't love you or enjoy the hug. But sometimes they have built a protective wall around themselves and this doesn't allow them to fully free their energy up. They probably aren't aware of it but the huggee does feel it. We Angels are not judging a person if they are a little repressed. We know that in order to understand why the hug felt like it did and to understand that these people are just as worthy of love as the next one. They may have had abuse in their lives and so have intimacy issues. This then shows in their energy and aura. They withhold a little of themselves when hugging due to the protective boundary they've put up. They want to do the right thing be emoting but don't realise they aren't really 'feeling' the hug. This is ok and they will find their way home themselves. They are no less than you as We are sure you know and they have their own journey towards love to experience. Bless them.

Having a hug is the perfect way to feel someone's love for you. So are strokes and pats and the best way is a kiss. Again it is an energy exchange and in order to really demonstrate to someone how much you love them is to enter their energy space as well as letting someone to do that to you. When someone comes in close to you this way you can sense where they are at and if you are truly intuitive you will pick up their emotional state and what they are going through. This is not a strange thing to do as animals do it to each other to assess friend from foe. They sniff each others breath to see what the energy is like coming from the other creature. They can sense dominance and passivity all through the energy fields. It's like a personal imprint.

Most animals are very tactile and express their love through grooming one another. It's an important demonstration of love and a social activity. Dogs are man's best friend and boy does he know how to show it. He licks and snuggles and jumps up for attention. He shows loyalty and protectiveness. There are no mediating thoughts or dysfunction. They run on pure animal instinct and react naturally to love given to them.

Any dysfunction is usually because of how he is treated by man. Cats are another animal who is very social and also show love through tactile means. They rub up against you and 'talk' to you. There's no doubt that domesticated animals are a great source of love and can certainly show you how to love fully. When you have a pet there is no threat there of abusive behaviour and there is total unconditional love. There are physical positives for having a loving pet. People's blood pressure goes down as do the stress levels. Imagine how less stressful life would be if you could let love in like this.

That is probably why a lot of you have animals as pets.

To feel love as purely and intensely as an animal does means you need to drop pretences and guards. This is not so easy to do due to your conditioning and distrust.

That by no means you are incapable of love because you ARE love. We love you. God loves you. It is possible to love despite what you have been through. We know and see your troubles and give as much support as We can. Some of you have such pain and have lost touch with the source of love within you, which is, of course, your God-source. It's not your fault and We love you no less. It is a part of your journey in this lifetime. And once you realise We are walking alongside you and nothing can sway our loyalty to you. We are aware that as We talk to you We may sound distant and not descriptive enough. We have been trying Our best to communicate with you through Lisa and We feel she is doing a great job. Words just don't seem to do justice to what We feel for you and what We are trying to impart. You'll just have to take Our word for it when We tell you We are around you. At least until you open up and feel Us. Once you open up and do this you will feel Us and this book will make a whole lot of sense.

It's not that hard. You are only limited by your thoughts and beliefs. So be daring, think outside the square.

Your life will be enriched so much if you do this and walk with Us Angels. We want so much for you to acknowledge Us and embrace Us. If you are aware of the main Arch Angels you will be aware of Our specific roles. If not there are many a book on Angelology out there and there are so many other Angels. In Heaven there are infinite numbers of Angels and the Arch Angels are major ones. There are hierarchies within the Angelic realm and all have jobs of their own. Some have roles looking after whole worlds. Others look after just the people on Earth.

We all have one purpose and that is to do God's will. We haven't got human qualities because We are not human in nature. But We do feel what you feel and can relate in ways you understand as it is an expression of love.

We can feel joy and happiness and understand your sense of humour. Laughter, as We've said before, is a great conductor of love and of course We understand this. That is why We have a sense of humour. Although it is translated into ways that makes sense to you. We have an important job to do and most of the time are serious. However the energy you produce when you laugh is attractive to Us Angels and We laugh and love along with you. We revel in the energy produced by your laughter and see the love emitted as it is produced this way.

When you are in a relationship you may know what it's like to be loved. You may have found your 'soul mate'. The love produced from this union is wonderful and intoxicating. Love is intoxicating anyway. And it is craved so much that the chocolate industry is making a small fortune (Ha! Ha!: Lisa). Love works wonders. It makes people go to extraordinary lengths for their loved ones and anything seems possible when love is involved. When your child wins an award at school and you see them collect it at their assembly don't you feel that swell in your chest of pride and love. You would die defending your children as your love for them is that strong. Love permeates through all else and it prevails over adversity. Love is surely a very powerful emotion

To illustrate how you feel love We want to discuss the feeling of lack of love. We want to address the issues you have had from your upbringing. Some of you have been scarred by your upbringing and you may be affected now as a result of it. If your parents had trouble showing you love or affection. If they were abusive and hostile. If they neglected you or blamed you and treated you as a scapegoat then you have experienced a lack of love. They may have shown you some love but this is cancelled out by all the other stuff they do to the contrary. Talking about this is not about blame so much as it is about demonstration.

To be made a scapegoat or black sheep of your family shows a deficiency somewhere in the love department and transference of pain. In other words you've inherited your family's pain because they can't deal with it themselves. It's like a virtual hot potato. You have to carry it for them. If they were capable of fully loving you or anyone they would protect you not pass it on to you. Like We've said before, We are not demonising these people as they are beautiful children of God themselves. We love them because this behaviour shows that they need all the love they can get. However We don't condone them not taking responsibility for their actions or them not learning their lessons. But We are here to talk about you not them as We will see to them another time. This is about our discussion with you and how you can appreciate the love you DO have when it's contrasted against the lack.

For those of you who suffered at the hands of ones who should have loved you unconditionally We need you to see what the lack of love looks like. This will make you appreciate and recognise what love actually does look like.

Even if your family did love you but didn't show it it still had the effect on you as if they didn't. You truly felt unloved and unrespected and that needs validating by Us saying We witnessed it and agree with you. We know that there is another side to this but We are currently focussing on your view of things which is just as valid. Despite the other party's intentions, good or bad, the end result was one of you feeling unloved and unappreciated. It also doesn't help if these people don't own their part in it and compounds any problems you may have resolving issues you have with them. It perpetuates your feeling of being unloved and unworthiness. From your perspective you feel that they are hostile to you and resent your very existence. Whether this is true or not is not the issue here, but how it makes you feel is. You are affected by others actions and it can be debilitating. This does not remove love from your life, it displaces it. When you have been that low you appreciate so much more the positive emotions demonstrated by a new love who is not a product of the environment you came out of. To finally find love after what you've been through shows how you are always able to love again. And be on the receiving end also. To feel like you've been to hell and back and finally finding love reinstates faith and trust in God because you relish the good emotions instead of taking it for granted.

Love is the antithesis of fear and when you have been in a fearful relationship such as abusive ones, love seems illusive and possibly non-existence. Let Us reassure you. Love never goes away and can be reinstated when you realise you are worthy of it. If you have a connection with Us Angels throughout this your faith in Us will buoy you and keep you afloat. That means Our love is getting through to you. It's up to you whether you tune in or not. Why not? We don't bite. People lose faith and say 'Is that all there is?' and throw the towel in before they've really get to know Us and learn how to utilize Us. This is because they expect bells and whistles and a golden light and orchestral music. This is unrealistic and a little indulgent. Get real. We rarely announce Ourselves to you this way. We have better things to do with Our energy. Such as communicating with you. It defeats the purpose to put on a grand display and We would rather get on with the job at hand.

To feel Our love just talk to Us. Either out loud or in your head. Don't worry We always hear you. You need to listen and trust your intuition as to Our response. Some of you who have clear hearing will hear Our voices. Those who are visual may get an image in your mind's eye. Those who have a 'knowing' will just 'know' what we are saying.

Whichever way that works for you We will accommodate.

As long as there is a connection and you're aware of it. Just entertained the possibility that We are there and that you can talk to Us. Act 'as if' and lo and behold you will open up. It's different to what you may expect it to be and also a lot easier than you think. It is probably so easy that you'd think it is too good to be true. Let the emotional responses We send you wash over you and take it on board. If you ask the question 'Will everything be alright in my relationship?' And you wait for a response then that response may come back as a confidence and blissful radiance wash over you and filling you up from behind your navel. Goose bumps are another indicator that what you feel We are saying is true or that We are around. Lisa laughs when she feels Our energy as it stirs up joy and bliss within her. She still has difficulty living in a human body as a lot of you do but the brief glimpses she gets from Us sustain her till the next time. If you felt Our energy in its fullest and purest form you would be blown away. So We only give you glimpses so that you can manage it. It is just that Our energy is a lot more potent than you are used to and We dilute it so that We don't overload you. It would detract from our purpose.

You are in denser bodies than We are. This is not a bad thing by no means. You are greatly admired for taking an Earthly assignment. You are powerful in your own right. There is no right or wrong, better or worse in this universe. So stop worrying about a non-issue. All that you are doing is creation. You are creating as you go and essentially all comes full circle back to love. We love you because We love always. All is love as are you. As are We. It permeates through everything and where there is a seeming lack of love We will be right there to balance it out. Your Earthly existence does have hardships and trials but it also has a lot of positives.

Like those who live in third world countries love each other and are at pains to deal with their poverty and disease. But they have each other and don't have a lot of material goods except the clothes on their backs and the ramshackle huts. They lose close family members to illness because there is no money for doctors and in some cases there are no medical assistance. Yet these people still feel and love and have dreams. They are very rich despite their poverty. They are gentle people with ready smiles. Friendly and welcoming. Love still exists despite hardships. Sometimes it is all one has.

Love is what makes the world around as the saying goes and it comes in many guises. Learn from your children as they are sent to teach you love before you ingrain them with conditioning. Turn it around and let them be the teachers. You underestimate these wonderful little ones. Children should not 'be seen and not heard'. How demeaning. Would you like that put on you? Of course not as it would make you feel worthless. So why do it to your children?

Love them with all your heart and soul. They deserve it as they give it to you freely. Remember you were all children once too and loved unquestioningly like them until you became conditioned and influenced by your elders. Despite their experience and wisdom those elders are moulded and shaped according to sometimes dysfunctional familial guidelines. The idea of what love is sometimes is distorted. Albeit will intended. This can inadvertently cause distress on young ones and they slowly become trained to behave that way and distance them further from their God-source.

They know it's natural to act from love but it is squashed when an adult deems it inappropriate. This causes harm to their sensibilities and distorts their already pure, unadulterated belief system. They need love much more than criticism.

We are focussing on the lack of love in order to illustrate how to know when you have it or you don't. In doing this We will lead you to opt for love and to appreciate what you recognise in what We say. We hopefully have shown the dark in order to emphasise the light. If you can see what detracts from you obtaining love then it will help you from doing it. Instead turning it around and doing the opposite – encouraging love. Nurturing love. Attracting love. Love in all its forms. Romantic love or familial love or love of your children. It is shown in a variety of ways in order to reach all of you. Because all of you have different needs and environments We want you to find it in the many ways it is expressed.

Artwork, music, theatre brings out the love in people as it touches directly the heart. When people express through an art form they are using their right brain. This is the intuitive and more emotive side of the brain. You feel more at home and yourself when you express through this means. This is akin to self-love and let's face it those who are renowned for their creative pursuits are passionate about it and that equals to love of their artform.

When you do what you love you get a glimpse of how happy you could be. How happy you can always be. When you're in touch with your God-source. That from which you originate. For when you are in touch with this you are truly yourself and that is love incarnate.

You ARE LOVE. Don't let others tell you otherwise.

God wants for you to make the journey through your life to find your way back home and along the way accumulate the experiences of love that you have had. There will always be highs and lows. You have to navigate them and learn to be flexible yet strong and firmly grounded.

Love is what you make it and if you decide to let it in you will be rewarded infinitely. It may seem elusive and unobtainable but remember there is love from within and love from God.

You also have Us Angels and We will do everything We can to bridge the gap.

If you want to perceive a lack of love in your life without looking at the alternatives then go right ahead and deny yourself bliss. It may take a little effort to reach Us but it is worth the time and motivation. It shouldn't be an effort as that is a man-made perception. It was a struggle for Lisa and still is. As she types this for Us she doubts what is being dictated. She is hoping that she makes sense. But she forgets that it is Us not her who writes this. She fluctuates in and out of belief and disbelief. She should know better. But again she needs the contrast to appreciate the lesson. When she makes the effort to link up with Us to write for Us it flows. As soon as she doubts she stops and procrastinates. When you tap into Us and God-source there is no effort. What takes effort is the doubting and procrastination. But you attribute that to the act of loving and so are easily deterred.

Tapping into love is like tapping into an inexhaustible energy source. It's how to get it that you perceive as hard. It's not hard. It's the act of leaving behind the known yet dysfunctional way of being that you are used to that is hard.

We are now sounding like an advertorial for love are We not?(giggle: Lisa).

Love is eternal as is Our love for you and We were humbled to have this chance to share Our thoughts with you.

Thanking you for being you and stay who you are but do it in the light of God. You cannot go wrong with Him. Thankyou Lisa, Our loved one, for allowing Us to work through you and it has been an absolute pleasure to share your energy. You are special.

With love and light to you all.

Gabriel

Thankyou to Gabriel. Believe me the pleasure was all mine.

I am so honoured to have this mighty Angel trust in me and work through me with this information. It has been an amazing journey to write this book and has opened my eyes to how much love is available to all of us. Boy are we lucky to have such a support team. I did have some difficulty with some issues that was discussed as they hit a nerve. I am actually a quiet, unassuming person and not wanting the attention that the book might bring. It is not me that is talking but Arch Angel Gabriel who is relaying the information. I had to really get my head around that one.

He (I relate to Gabriel as male but as was said earlier Angels are androgynous) is the Angel of communication after all. It seems love is a commodity of which is valuable yet readily available. I have been guilty of denying myself it sometimes and boy does it hurt to have a lack of it. But essentially I realised I contributed to the problem by my being obstructive and stubborn. Stubbornly refusing love because I didn't think I was worthy. Writing this book has been cathartic for me as I connected with Gabriel I actually experienced the phenomenal love that the Angels, and God of course, have for all of us. It just IS. It just IS there and is never ending. I could see how love runs through everything that exists on every realm. It is so reassuring to know that and the love they give is addictive. Don't just take my word for it, try it yourself.

I am by no means an expert at this and don't wish to sound arrogant. I hope I sound like I'm sharing this experience with you. As you can see Love is an important emotion and to have a book that talks all about it is a blessing in itself. Heaven knows our world need as much love as we can get. I have felt the unconditional love of an Angel and realise how dysfunctional I have been in the past. Especially regarding the field of love. I mistook it for possession and ownership. I got angry when it was taken away from me and hated myself because I thought I had done something stupid to drive it away. I didn't realise that it wasn't meant to be in that form. I didn't trust enough that I would find it again. Now I know I have the love of God and the Angels I don't need for love externally any more. But it will be a bonus if it does happen. It's taken all my life (39 years) to figure it out. It still doesn't mean I've perfected it but I certainly feel a bit more relaxed about it than I used to. I have my son who is love itself. He is an endless source of joy to me and has taught me a lot about love and how selfish I was as a young adult. I was self-absorbed and taken with my career and social scene. Then I met my son's father and we had our son. Although his father and I are no longer together and our love waned our son is the greatest source and teacher of love that we have experienced. Children force you to love unconditionally and boy do they! Not because they are selfish but because they are totally dependent on you and reward you with unconditional love and adoration. You learn that you would move Heaven and Earth for them and their happiness. You learn sacrifice. You learn to be humble because you are totally depended upon and have to clean up messes that have a pint sized cause.

It is a love that is rich in rewards and benefits. You are filled with pride at their first step and their first word. You are filled with apprehension when they go to school for the first time and yet recognise their growth.

This is how I imagine God and the Angels must feel about us and our progress. They want to love us so much, or rather they DO love us so much. Yet like a parent they hold back because they know we won't learn anything if they do it all for us. They have stressed that they are there if we need them but can't live our lives for us.

I hope that what has been said here is of use to you and I hope it is not the one and only time we meet. It has been so enjoyable to share this experience with you as you are surely worth it and deserving of love.

Love always
Lisa

Wisdom of Children – Words from Gabriel

Wisdom of Children – Words from Gabriel
(dedicated to my son, my light, my Robert Ray)

Introduction

Hello there. It's been six years since I wrote both The Wisdom of Love and The Wisdom of Children. A lot has happened and my son has grown up to be a strapping six foot tall 17 and a half year old. He is now driving and living with his dad. I am revising the old work and since have written the third book in this trilogy with yet more books to come. I am working in my own business as a professional psychic medium on a well-known psychic line and am studying Naturopathy. I am still teaching belly-dance and aiming to get back into my illustration.

I have started holding spiritual chat nights and channelling nights too where I channel Arch Angel Gabriel. My son is a gentle giant and is as grounded as much as being a Cancerian can let him be. However he is my grounding source and a total joy to me as he is a good young man with a good moral compass. He usually keeps me in line and on the straight and narrow. I have lost one budgie and gained a new one. We have had a goldfish but he passed too. As you can see I am an animal lover. And unfortunately as of this week we are without the dog. She passed away at the ripe old age of thirteen.

My now expertise at being a mum is being shown in how my son was raised and even he attributes his level headedness and savvy to my raising him. His father and I, even though separated, have raised him relatively consistently with each other. He is a credit to his father also. I have learnt through the act of parenting how our children do need both parents, and most importantly both parents who actually communicate and work together. Our sons do need their fathers as well as their mothers and visa versa for girls. They need a male and a female role model. Listening to them instead of saying that they should be seen and not heard as that old saying goes. Yes we need to teach them manners and respect but seriously how can that be done with violence in smacking and verbal harshness? We need to show firmness yet with love and respect for our children and my beautiful son, thank goodness, has the ability to show respect to others. He was shown respect and he gave it back.

I have made mistakes too and sometimes find it hard to judge what to let go and what to pursue. However my son has helped me to parent him because of our bond and the fact that his upbringing was relatively calm. As I mentioned, I did make mistakes and by no means am I perfect. However I have found that if I am firm but calm my child got the message and ended up working 'with' me instead of against me. I think my being a mum of only one did help. Even though he has step and half siblings. I have so much respect for mums who have more than one. Boy that's a tough job. I take my hat off to you. I am one of three siblings. I know how hard it must have been to my mum to juggle all of us. The extended family helps too.

Children are our future as that song goes and we need to treasure them and nurture them. Bless them with a lot of laughter and love and full bellies. When you chastise them do it with love and with options to pull themselves up so that they can learn appropriate self-management skills. Children can become confused by our anger and it can create future dysfunction that could be avoided.

I have had such joy in writing each of these books and look forward to future instalments and hope to see you again. Please enjoy the following and thankyou for your readership.

Blessed Be
Lisa

WISDOM OF CHILDREN

There I was minding my own business, watching television quite contentedly, when I had a thought pop into my head that seemed like spirit trying to contact me. It had been about six weeks since I finished my first book called Wisdom of Love – Words from Gabriel. I had written the book in just under two weeks which was amazing. I felt glued to the computer and wasn't allowed to leave it except to do ordinary things such as eat, attend to my son's and my needs and to sleep.

Apparently I was to start writing the next instalment and I know that there is at least another one to come. This book, I was told, is to do with children and their influence on society and visa versa. I already knew that this book was to be written but didn't realise it would have to be done so soon. I just kept getting subtle hints from spirit to do so and procrastinated because I had a lot of Earthly chores to do first. Thankfully spirit is patient and understanding. I gathered Gabriel had not finished his message to us humans and he was on a roll. He certainly has the gift of the gab. I always thought I was a chatterbox but boy was I out done when Gabriel showed up.

I always try to keep a level head on my shoulders and in no way do I have tickets on myself that I am anything special. I do not feel or believe that I am better than anyone else. I also laughed when told I was to channel a book with Gabriel. Me? Lisa? Yerright! Only other people do that. People who are famous channels or psychics are the ones who write books channelled from beings greater than us. I work as a psychic medium and have got some beautiful, loyal clients who make it so easy to read and let spirit come through. Still, despite eight years of doing this still didn't prepare me for the role of author. I truly did not feel I was qualified for the role. Still I grapple with it. But I figure it's just like talking to a friend, which is what you are.

Besides, it's not necessarily me that is talking. I am, after all, just a conduit. I didn't believe I could write the last book and yet it came so easily that it was done in two weeks! I have had many other projects on the go such as illustrations for a friend's book, helping build stock for my other friends craft stall, study and also just being a mum. House work? Hah! Forget it! I manage the basics. After being in our home for six years, which is the longest I've ever been in one spot, I have accumulated a lot of things and have a supply of stuff which would cater to at least three garage sales. That's beside the point. I have many other priorities and mine and my son's happiness is one of them.

We have a house full of animals. We have three cats, a budgie, one dog, a goldfish and in recent times a rabbit, mouse and guinea pigs. We lost both the rabbit, guinea pigs and mouse to natural causes and the year before I had to have my beloved 31 year old horse Buddy put down. I believe that animals bring a lot of joy and we have a house full of joy. They are our family and being a single mum, family is all important. We love our animals and they love us. They hang around us because our house is full of laughter (usually at my expense) and that raises vibrations.

When I tune in to do readings or to write these books Rosie, tortoise shell cat, sits curled up on or near my lap. So does Casper our white kitten. They just adore the energy that comes through and want to be as close as possible to me when I channel as the energy is calming and peaceful not to mention healing. My son sits at the end of the bed and is usually very placid and relaxed whilst I write this book on my laptop. He is a very aware little soul. Well not so little anymore. He is twelve and almost as tall as me. He is almost my height which is five foot six and is a strong, solid boy who is a gentle giant in his own class at school. He knows his own strength and yet is kind and considerate towards others. He knows the little squirt at school who teases him is no match for him and deals with those issues with humour and wit. He knows he could dangle quite easily the kid by his ankle but he chooses not to. His intuitive way of solving problems at school has been noticed and praised by his teachers at school and is called a good role model for his peers and those younger than him at school.

My son is also in his last year of primary school and starts high school next year. This will be a test of his character and he knows it. He is almost adult like in his demeanour and understands the psychology behind other kid's behaviour. Still he knows that he needs to toughen up and get ready for the pre-adult world. He, like many children nowadays, is intuitive and very 'knowing'. I have had to teach him stamina and protection. And although he knows what I do for a living he is sheltered from it as life has to be balanced and 'normal'. I have not taught him how to be intuitive, he has got it already and quite naturally and organically. He is sensitive to 'visiting' spirits and just knows what is going on when I tune in. This way I have to be careful because when I open up to read for someone whilst he is around I have to keep the energy contained. As children grow and get older they become more conditioned to society and it's closed minded attitudes to the metaphysical side of things. They close down and become engrossed in the physical. Which has its benefits. But can stunt another's development and make them feel unappreciated and unaccepted. Especially if they want to follow a metaphysical path. We shouldn't make people or children feel like they are wrong for being naturally intuitive as this can disarm them of the tools that can help them survive in the world.

This book, I feel, is to help colour in details about these qualities in our little ones. And to learn how to integrate them into everyday life and normality. We need to promote awareness to overcome the ingrained ignorance and misinformation from those who really aren't qualified to say whether or not this kind of thing exists. All children are born, I believe, naturally intuitive. All animals have it and use it as it comes naturally to them. It's a natural instinct and sense just like the sense of smell. They have to use it in order to survive and as a way of avoiding danger. I have learnt so much from spirit about parenting intuitively and not denying it in my son despite concerned looks from my parents and well-meaning people. But I couldn't drum it out of him even if I had wanted to. Which I don't by the way. From a young age he has been very wise and knowing and also been able to see spirit. He would say things such as that he knew what the man I was going to marry would look like and that he would have a little sister (who now exists). I would neither encourage nor deny this ability in him as I wanted him to decide for himself if he would allow this in himself. He now is a well-adjusted and calm boy who keeps me grounded with his common sense and wisdom. Sometimes it feels like I'm the kid and he is the parent.

We have to honour these wise young ones and trust that they are here for a reason. To teach us not the other way around. The Angels know this and want to talk to you about it as now is the time to shed old, outdated belief systems which stunt the development and growth of these little blessings. Decades, if not centuries, of narrow minded, fear based conditioning needs releasing and transformed into clear thinking and understanding. If I had not been intuitive myself I may have felt pressure from family and others to force my son into these very limited beliefs that have their basis in fear and ignorance. Probably due to some religious and politics from long ago. Those who are in that conditioning don't realise that they have been controlled and brainwashed by those who seem to be in positions of esteem and respect. That is why we need to think for ourselves and not conform all the time. Children know this. They know that to conform is not the way to live life. It is restricting and limiting to God's plan for us. I love children and am so proud of my best achievement, which is my son. He teaches me so much and I listen to him because sometimes his clear vision is unadulterated by conditioning and unhealthy perceptions. He cuts through the crap and tells me as he sees it. I get caught up in my programming and flounder about struggling with an issue and he steps in and says 'Why don't you…..?'. I am astounded constantly in his faith in me and that is enough to make me take on the world. I have dutifully written down eight chapter headings a few days ago and have put them aside trusting that Gabriel has a plan as to how this book will go. I don't have any influence in what Gabriel wants to say except my limited vocabulary. He (I see Gabriel as a Him even though many see Gabriel as a She) wants us to reel in the beauty and the innocence of our little ones and see how to learn from them. Instead of them being 'seen and not heard' as that old saying goes. He wants us to recognise that these children are pure love and untouched by dysfunction. They are clean slates as it were. Just because they are brand new and untainted does not diminish their potential wisdom. We underestimate them and push them to one side as if their views are naïve and uneducated.

The Angels know what potential is secreted away within these little ones and want to enlighten us. I, for one, will surely learn a lot of that I am positive. Here I am writing this book and the journey to get here is phenomenal. If you had mentioned to me ten years ago that I would be writing a book and working as a psychic I would not have believed you. So I shall now hand the laptop and the book over to Gabriel and only hope I can do justice to his intended message. God bless.

Gabriel

Hello my beautiful ones. You are so loved. You are so loved because you ARE God's children. Isn't that how you all start out? We Angels do God's work constantly and in all our travels and assignments We cannot go past the fact that you are God's creation and so are seen as His children. Do you not all start out as children? Do you not remember the pure joy of running in the green, green grass as the sun shone down and into the arms of your loved ones? The blatant trust that they will catch you? That is how We want you to now remember and do with Us Angels. In this way can you lean from your children? OUR children. Each other. For, as you have undoubtedly heard before you are still God's children and always will be. Why poo poo the value of your little ones? 'Because they lack experience' you say? Nonsense! They have lifetimes of experience as do you. In fact the knowledge they DO have is unadulterated, unlike many of you who have conditioned yourselves into being fully limited in your thinking processes and have conditioned yourselves into being fully limited in your thinking processes and beliefs. We do not intend to insult you but merely be objective as to how We portray you. You are all loveable and worthy. Just a little misguided by your peers and mentors.

Children have yet to take on your conditioning and are clear of any dysfunction and misinformation. They see things exactly as they are. This then frees them up to think clearly and communicate clearly. Sometimes too clearly for some of you and so you try to suppress it in them because it's too confrontational for you. Why hide from the truth? It will come right back at you and bite you (as Lisa would say) on the butt!

These little ones know it's healthy to live now and in the moment. For worrying of looking to the past or future is a little like the pause button on your TV remotes. You go nowhere fast! Like being on a complicated freeway intersection and constantly missing the turn off because you are too stubborn to relinquish control of the steering wheel. Your blinker is permanently stuck on 'left'. And around and around you will go until you get it right. Problem then is the road rage kicks in and you start yelling at God to let go of you as you are in control. Don't you see that God only wants the best for you and will never steer you wrong? Yield to God and He can steer you safely off that wretched freeway.

Children know how to yield but you keep telling them they are wrong. Can't you see you are setting them up for problems in the future? Why not let them be brave and take risks? Wrapping them in cotton wool or restricting them because of your own fears is not giving them life skills. Skills which will help them to survive long after you are gone. Are you arrogant enough to believe that you are all that they need? That they can't survive without you or your very existence? We know you mean well and believe you have their best interests at heart, however they have THEIR lives to lead and you can't take that away from them. They knew coming into this life that there would be certain conditions with it. They agreed to take them on. They are your equal and do not need telling how to live their lives. You are there to set an example. To teach by example. To love by example. We trust you implicitly even when you stray off course. We do, however, have to sound harsh in order to make Our point. Try to take it on the chin. After all you are Our Loved Ones. You are equally loved and Our bluntness is equal to and same strength as Our love for you. Even as We speak Lisa is struggling to type as her own beloved child hovers behind her. And she has pushed him away as he has irked her. She is getting stressed due to his energy levels overlapping onto hers and distracting her from this job. We gently point out to her that this is an example and that she is squashing, inadvertently, the eagerness to please and love of her little one. She, herself, does what We ask of you, yourself, to contain. We judge her not. Merely We point out what may perpetuate her anxiety and how to prevent it from spilling over into her young one's energy field. It is about prevention as opposed to blame. We love Lisa and do not criticise. She is laughing now as it dawns on her what We are trying to convey. She did not trust her young one to respect what it was she was doing when in fact he knows fully and with great respect wanted to be a part of it. She assumed he was not capable of understanding what it was she was writing and even now protests as We make her write this last statement. She loves him body and soul but does what a lot of you do and that is to assume. You assume that a child's mind is incapable of spiritual thought. Incapable of spiritual understanding or concept. Yet this very child has taught her so much as she will tell you. He is very perceptive and keen. Also he is very loving and kind. His heart's yearning is for her to be with him. She always is distracted. Her conversations with him fleeting. All because she is immersed in procrastination by reading books or talking to others. She is tired because she doesn't take proper care of herself. She is caught up in being 'grown up'. He lovingly obeys her when she asks for peace. He is slowly starving of the attention that quite frankly he deserves. Again We are not angry at Lisa but are trying to illustrate how many of you treat your children and that this could be prevented. Lisa IS a good mother. But she is only human. It is a common phenomenon. Lisa is lost in her own life's process and does not mean to affect her little one this way. She adores and worships him. She is trying to juggle things. This is what all of you do, no?

You may have been treated the same way by your own parents or caregivers. The world you have created is fast paced and hurried. How can you teach by example? How to love or live if you are only living a half-life yourself? You always look to other adults for validation and common sense and disregard what your little ones say. Sometimes the simplest and most exacting comment comes from a child's mouth. Purely because they have uncensored minds. What comes from God comes from the pure mind and mouth of a young one. You spend too much time forcing your perceptions, beliefs and attitudes on them and punish them when they veer from them and go it alone. They are individuals with their own opinions and perspectives.

The key here is purity. Purity of feelings. Purity of intention. You are born this way and then lose it as your elders condition you. We Angels know you mean well and by no means want to be harsh towards you. We just want you to be REAL. Love is the means by which you can have purity. Love is an energy. Almost like a currency. You give love, you receive love. True love is like electricity. It travels as an energy source and carries with it intentions. Your intentions. It is what sustains you and nourishes you. When you forget to love you tend to lose your way and yet you don't realise until it's too late. Or so it seems. For it is never too late to repent as it has been said before and you can always turn to the light. Don't be stubborn and look the other way because you believe YOU know what is good for you. As you grow physically you tend to grow away from God because you believe he doesn't exist or at least exists only as a theory or construct. You think that you'll be a believer another day because you're too busy right now. Why do this? Why not include God in your life? He can only enhance your life and He is after all your Father. Do you not realise that with God in your life the pure love source that is He who is almighty drives you effortlessly and with accurate precision. He is impenetrable and unflappable. We tell you this as THIS is how to lead by example. This is how your children already behave but you are too caught up to notice. And if you must lead by example then this is a way We Angels suggest.

If you have purity or intention and absolute belief in the power of God then you won't be swayed easily from the true path. It is when you doubt that the energy drains from you and you believe you are forsaken. It is not God or Us who have forsaken you. You only perceive it as such and so abandon your mission thinking there is no point in continuing because the feeling has left you. If the feeling has left you then you are defeated. Can you see how you let yourself down by doubting? All you have to do is pick up where you left off. The 'mission' hasn't left you, it is still active and if you treat it as if there's a pause button all you have to do is resume. It's like a temporary veil put across your eyes. The 'mission' is still there you just think it's gone. Be strong. Be persistent and refuse to allow a simple veil to obscure your vision and aim. Pull that veil away in order to see and resume your 'mission'.

As children you did so but with years of conditioning and warped belief systems you may have been forced to adopt, you lose your way. There is a language that religious people speak that seems foreign to most people and these people label it as 'whacko' or 'obsessive'. However when you are a part of it it makes plenty of sense. In some cases it's the language of love. No We are not getting all romantic on you. We just wish to explain that there is no harm in what these people do if it doesn't infringe upon you. Let them behave as such. For they have found their Christ. No matter what religion they belong to, the energy is the same regardless of the label. Christ energy is just the pure energy of God. It is the intermediary between Him and you. It is what worked through Jesus. That is why He was – IS – the

Christ. There are many religions and experiences in your world that have their own belief systems and structures. They have their own terminology but essential the message is Love. Children are embodiments of God's Love. When We say this you may be thinking We refer to your little ones. No Loved Ones. We refer to you also. Remember? You are God's children too and in your maturing you forget that because your aim is to 'grow up' and become self-sufficient. You leave behind your direct connection to the love which is God. For that is what He is – Love.

Are children loved by God?

Yes, Loved Ones, children are loved. Just as you yourself are loved. This heading may seem a silly question but We are illustrating a point. To say that a child is not loved by God is to say that God does not exist. Don't forget you are a child of God yourself. Do you not believe you, yourself, are worthy of love? If you don't then We feel you would perceive an absence of God in your life. That is not to say He doesn't exist for He does. Just that you perceive He doesn't. And so experience life as God-less. Which then perpetuates your belief system that you're alone and without value. When you let God into your life you find that all are of value, including yourself. That is what God is all about. If you are a parent you'll understand the value of setting a good example for your little ones. If you are down so are they. Your little ones are barometers for you to see the climate of the family environment. They reflect you and your moods. If you are suffering they are suffering. Literally! If you're happy and confident then invariably so are they.

God flows through all of you, it's just that some of you aren't tuned in or aware of it. Children ARE aware of it but eventually become conditioned to deny that aspect of themselves which is innate. You reconstruct God's plan to how YOU see fit and then wonder afterwards why it doesn't work as well as first thought. You bemoan that God is never there or never listens and your children see this and try to help. Only problem is you don't always listen and tend to dismiss it as childish fantasy. Meanwhile the hole you're digging keeps getting bigger and deeper. A whole new meaning to 'light at the end of the tunnel' no?

The whole point of this chapter is to describe to you how to love like children do. Like God does. For it is the same. All you have to do is believe. Believe you are God's children. You ARE God. To know that God loves

His children means you do believe. It means you Love God and trust in Him. It also means you see what He stands for and is. Pure Love. You are pure Love. For you have the God energy within you. So to love God is to love yourself. As simple as that. Oh and God does so love you all. Look in your hearts and see that child who needs only love to survive. For if you were to truly look into that innocent child's heart you will see that you deserve to be loved. And to give love too. To be able to give love means you have discovered that you are worthy of receiving. For when you realise you deserve love you then allow it to be given to you. And in turn you are able to give love because your reserves are topped up. Can you now see how love is an exchange of energy? As soon as you allow it to flow through you like a current, you can then pass it on to another as if you have plugged into them. Just like electricity.

It is like a rat maze inside your brain (excuse the analogy. I'm sure Gabriel is leading to something here. Lisa). There are plenty of passage ways to manoeuvre but at the end of one or two there is a blockage. This is like you stopping the flow of love by just thinking in an ineffectual way. As soon as you lift that blockage the sooner love can flow through and you will realise that there is such a thing as love. In children there are no blockages but with learnt behaviours gradually those walls go up and they believe that it's hard work to love and so stunt their capacity to love. It's a self-perpetuating vicious cycle. It then becomes what is known as habit. We Angels bemoan the fact that you humans are creatures of habit. You find one thing that works and because you don't feel brave enough to be free thinkers and fly by the seat of your pants (as Lisa puts it) which is how life should be lived (creatively not predictively), you use that one thing and use it as a template.

You fear abandonment. By your family and your peers. You perceive that it is something that you have done so you try to find the behaviour 'button' that works and put it on repeat. You repeat a behaviour when around others that you know works and so remain static and predictable. Predictable is good, but is not challenging and there is no learning. You are participating in fear based behaviour. Fear of failure and of doing the wrong thing. Of not being acceptable. Not conforming. For to not conform equates to pain for some of you and instead of working through that pain barrier you freeze and stop your skills at communication on that 'button' you so favour. And because your children (Our children) have no fear they do things you daren't. You pull them back and chastise them, Perpetuating a learnt belief that they are incompetent, untrustworthy and incapable. This slows them down considerably. They lose their dexterity and flexibility. They become SUPPRESSED.

It may seem like We are being harsh or critical. As We have said before it is not Our intention. We merely wish to convey how the lack you may feel of love in your life may be due to conditioning which stems from your own childhood environment. If you learn how your beliefs have been shaped and that it may stem from a deficit in love then you may see more clearly how to prevent the same deficit occurring in your own beloved children's lives. This is not about blame. Man finds it hard to be clearly and openly objective. Try as you might there is still a little defensiveness there and We Angels hope to chi at it and remove it so as to help you become clearer in your intent. Leave the blame behind and be as honest with yourself as you can be. We feel it comes down to your own lack of self-love. That is one reason why you are where you are. To experience love. To find love. To become love. AGAIN!!! For you were once pure love. Nay, you ARE still pure love. Because you come from pure love! You just don't know it let alone recognise it.

We have just pushed Lisa to write what We are trying to show her. She, of course, is writing on Our behalf. However all the same she is taking on board what We say. What We have shown her was aimed to help her in her time of need as she herself is going through the throws of self-evaluation. She is finally analysing her experiences and allowing herself to cry. These tears are presentative of her childhood pain which is coming to the fore because of old patterning she is forced to deal with. Some of this patterning is owned by her family and some is owned by herself. Oh that is hard for her to type. We are using her as an example to illustrate that you are all still the little children you were ten, twenty, fifty years ago. That you still deserve to be loved as that small child was so long ago.

Getting back to the point We were trying to make to Lisa, and so to you, is that as you think it so it shall be. Children know this and when they act it out you, as adults, call them naïve. You have so convinced yourself something so simple in theory must be bogus. Oh how cynical of you. Isn't it funny how, when in a crisis, you call for Us and when We come to give you help and advice you reject it because of it's simplicity? We, as Angels, revert to simplicity of love and how it conquers all that gets in its way. Who'd believe that these little ones ware stronger in faith and conviction than you adults? That they actually succeed in hitting their mark and jump with glee at their faith pulling them through? Do you envy their optimism but dare not show it? Why not be as they are? Don't sniff at the thought. For what We are driving at here is that very point. As with Lisa, who is not allowing Us to flow through her and as a result is constantly making typing errors. Her adult brain is interfering and not trusting that We are actually working through her. We make her read and reread this last passage to show her that it DOES make sense. If she lets it.

This leads Us to the topic at hand. 'Are children loved by God?'. All you have to do is to KNOW this and you will feel it. Feel it from memories of your childhood and the happy moments. Children know how to love God and in loving God they then love themselves. So as We said, if you think it so it shall be. To know that children are loved by God is to know that you are loved! Do you understand now?

Do children hear the voice of God?

Do you remember those times Lying in grass at a park or in your back yard? Do you remember concentrating really hard to see if you can figure out where heaven (up there) ends and Earth (down here) begins? Did your parents or siblings explain to you where God was believed to inhabit? Did this lead to those times in the garden talking to the benevolent being in the sky just to see if you got a response? This lasts only so long before you start to be informed that its not a good idea to be caught talking to yourself. That now God apparently doesn't exist and is just a being created to support a certain belief system. This may seem cruel and deceptive but it is man made in order to contain the unknown. What you deny can't possibly exist now can it? People have differing ideas as to what or who God is. That is why there are many religions in your world. As if you can own God and turn Him into what you want Him to be. You miss the point. He just IS. He was here long before any of you. He created you! You are eventually conditioned by society at a macrocosmic level, and family at a microcosmic level to believe all that you see is all that there is. So what do you do as a child verging on adulthood? You stop 'listening'. You start to rely on your own wits and cognitive processes. It needs to be visible to be real. Otherwise put it in the too hard basket.

You grow up and get diplomas in your field of expertise. You get a job, travel a bit, meet someone to love and settle down to have a family. Wait, We are going somewhere with this so please be patient. You stop in your tracks one day when your own child asks outright is there a God? What do you say? Obviously there are many contributing factors to consider. The country you live in and the religion (if any) that you adopt. The thing is these little ones already know that God exists and that He is within as opposed to without. They are only asking because you are of value to them and your validation is so important as to where they go from there. They are testing you to see if you hear Him too. They long to hear you say 'Yes God does exist. He lives in our hearts. I talk to Him too and He talks to me'. However, if you say the opposite, the little ones suppress the 'knowledge' in order to please and to conform. Heaven forbid should they be punished for even thinking such a thing. However, if you do support them, We Angels jump with joy for then you have opened a door to letting Us, and God, help you when you need help.

The little ones sing for no apparent reason other than being happy. They play with imaginary friends (or ARE they?) and talk to themselves unashamedly. Their hearts soar at the beauty of nature for God is in all that they see. Although they don't give God a name because to them He is more of a feeling than a concept or construct. He is that fluttery feeling when a colourful butterfly flies past and they long to capture it briefly to examine it. He is the feeling of warmth when their mother or father walks into a room after and absence. That is how they perceive God's presence and that He is all around. His energy runs through you and you recognise it as those flutters and warmth. The glow of love you may feel for loved ones is the energy of God flowing through you. As We have mentioned before, it is akin to electricity. You put it in – it exists. You don't – IT doesn't. Or seemingly doesn't. For love exists regardless. God is love so HE exists regardless. Regardless of your stubbornness. If you don't (as Lisa puts it) plug into Him of course you won't FEEL Him.

Those people who are born again Christians have suddenly 'plugged in' and surprise surprise FOUND Him!! He wasn't there before so why is He now? Because if you turn away from the heater you won't feel the warmth on your face. Now in blizzard conditions this is silly isn't it? These born again souls just made the effort to see if they could feel His presence and lo and behold are pleasantly surprised to find He has a warmth. He IS warmth. He IS love and is sitting patiently like a Christmas cracker (Lisa is suppressing laughter – another expression of God and love – at our terminology We love this so) on the table waiting to be pulled open and the goodness inside to be exposed. It is symbolic of you and that you were just to look inside you will see how all that you perceive as beautiful is an expression of God! Isn't that 'cool', as Lisa's son Robert would say?

God is that feeling of benevolence you feel when you allow your compassion to surface. When you comfort another as they cry and suffer. You open the flood gates and allow the warmth of your love for them to gush forth so that they feel it. So that you, in the hopes of easing their discomfort and pain, somehow transfer that warmth which is glowing from somewhere around the heart area to pass to them energetically. In the hopes that you can buoy them and heal them. This is an intuitive act not a cognitive act. In fact you probably don't twig straight away what you are doing. You try to transfer these feelings into words in order for the other party to know that you feel that way because, you think, how else are they going to know? It doesn't occur straight away to you that they can 'feel' your compassion. Not because you are at fault, but because you are not aware yet. You may not have learnt to tune into your intuition in order to sense this method of feeling and sharing God's energy. Those who work as healers and psychics have some idea.

Again We are not trying to put you down. From where We are We see all of you as equal but at differing stages and with different choices in life experiences. You all have something to learn from each other. We Angels are amazed at how you progress even against great odds! You are Our pride and joy and We walk with you every step of the way just as if you were toddlers taking your first steps. It is a proud moment indeed when you achieve your milestones. Lisa is joking with Us saying it's a pity We Angels don't have a digital camera! Oh but We DO! Every act, every thought is recorded in images or energies that We understand. We look at them with glee and love as We observe your lessons learnt. The feeling of love and being at one with God stems from centredness. As We discussed earlier about feeling others compassion, when you are centred and prepared to receive God's love you will feel the glow from within. All that is going on in the world will suddenly make sense to you. You see in your angry neighbour their righteousness and agree with it looking at their perspective and yet it won't affect your own. This is centredness. We laugh as Lisa has only just now seen where We were heading with this theory.

We ask 'What happened to trust Dear One?. To be unflinching in your resolve yet flexible enough to allow others their space and belief systems. To include all others without your own expense. Loyalty. To yourself as well as others at the same time. To hear all arguments but to retain your own whilst allowing anger to wash over you so you can make wise decisions. To give to others when all seems fully expended from your own resources. This is feeling God within you. It is compassion and stoicism all at once. It ultimately can be achieved efficiently when you are centred. Of course not all of you can be centred at once. You have life to live and the merry dances it takes you on. Don't worry you will come to it (centredness) eventually. It's only a matter of time. Allow it to come to you. However do not lose heart if you still don't experience it straight away. You may have to go through the upheavals you are experiencing right now first in order to grow. You, of course, can experience it any time you wish but you may have a few stages to go through before you feel it fully. This does not by any means show that you are unworthy. Remember YOU chose this life path and all the trials that come with it.

Your choices are to be respected. We Angels in no way will tamper with your life path choices. We are standing by to assist only and not to rob you of choices. You are working towards this ultimate point of centredness as this is exactly where you find God. When you access this goal you will feel a raised awareness and consciousness. There will be a feeling of absolute joy and buoyancy. Almost invincibility. Can you understand why We are talking about you and not necessarily just about children? It is because as children you did hear the voice of God. You arrive fresh and new from God's arms into your Earthly life and slowly uncoil to become a creation of which is in His likeness but make it on your own. If you stray from God's path you are not in the wrong but could be doing much better for yourself in endeavouring to stay with the program (as you say). You are designed to do God's work as a human. God wants you to individuate enough from Him so as to learn what it is you came to Earth to learn. You can always touch base with Him and devote your life's work to Him but We want you to be present and centred in your own identity enough to grow back towards God. This does not mean you are disconnected from God. Not at all. We do not mean that your true connection to God will hinder. Only your obsession with it will. If you obsess then you are not thinking for yourself and so will be going around and around in circles not getting to where God wants you to be – WHOLE.

As We said before, yield to God. By yield We mean give of yourself to His love and let it grace your life. However remain independent enough to be yourself if your beautiful human form. For isn't it wonderful to keep a secret? The worst kept secret in the world (We hear Lisa laugh at Us). That God is within you all. You don't need to advertise it like an evangelist. Although that in itself serves its purpose. It's not that you should not be proud of your love and connection to God. It's more of a state of 'being'. A serenity, if you will. To allow it to glow from within to show the world how beautiful it is to be with the Grace of God. This is how the children 'Hear the voice of God'. And so can you.

Children – Expression of God

What are We here for? We Angels love you and your children openly. That is one of the many reasons We are here. In fact it's the main reason. Lisa just said it is like you and We are joined at the hip. Now it is Our turn to laugh. Very apt We are thinking. However did you know that another reason for Our existence, We Angels, is as an expression of God. All that exists is an expression of God Almighty. For life is fluent with the language of God. You come forth into your existence as an expression of Him. He watches over you to ensure your safety and wellbeing. He even works through you as He does with Us. He works through you best when you are being creative. Have you noticed how uplifting some music can be? How the colours on a piece of artwork can capture your attention for quite some time? How the movement of dance makes you feel exhilarated and joyful? Have you also noticed how much your society puts value on anything other than these pursuits as though it has precedence over it and is less 'flaky'. Certainly most of you do put time aside for these pursuits but they are not taken as seriously as cognitive pursuits and the all important dollar. These pastimes, as you call them, are lower down on the priority list than materialistic needs. What a shame, We say, as it can so enrich your life much more than that new Porsche.

It boils down to attribution. What you have been taught to believe in is due to your conditioning and what your elders 'attributed' to a certain activity. "Ugh! Why would you listen to that? It's boring" they may say. So you attribute a feeling to that particular activity to remind you that it's supposedly 'boring'. When in actual fact deep down inside you feel entertained by it and long to pursue it. You have attributed a negative feeling towards it and so stop before you participate in order to appear as though you are conforming. And that is a big problem. Especially when children are small. They learn to 'attribute' a certain belief or feeling to something or someone simply because their parents do so and so they learn to suppress their own powers of judgement and intuitive 'knowing' because they are forced to conform. They are quite capable of attributing their own healthy, untainted beliefs and understanding of something or someone themselves. They just have to conform because they haven't yet got the skills to stand up to their elders. These children know it's healthy to individuate and form their own ideas but are pressured to conform in order to contain them. This is still needed to an extent purely for their own safety. However as they get older it becomes more of a hindrance to their development. Parents, We Angels understand, only do it out of love and quite rightly so. However at the first sing of independence in a child can scare the adults into overdrive. They forget that the wisdom of God runs through all of you including your children and that they are just as capable as you are.

Just notice the subtleties in their facial expressions when you tell them a sophisticated joke. They have a lot of potential to understand the intricacies of life. After all they have to start somewhere don't they? You did! Do you forget what it was like? To be brave enough to individuate and develop your own ideas about life. Then to have an elder put their two cents worth in because they assumed you had no idea what to do. It slows you down doesn't it? Your ability to deal with it is raring to go but then you have to stop to consider your elders point of view and BAM! You miss your golden opportunity. We are talking about energy transfer not whether it's right or wrong to guide your children. Children do need guidance and sometimes chastisement. However if you suppress them altogether it will effect energy levels and motivational drives. Your thoughts lead to feelings and from there your feelings uplift you or disable you. You are not different from your little ones and feel just as they do. To understand what We are driving at you need to engage your empathy.

Lisa points out that We Angels sound like We think you don't recognise to do this already. But of course We do and We are proud of you even more than usual when you do. As We are proud of you already for being you. We simply are asking you to engage an ability which is already innate in you. In order to do that We have to draw your attention to it and the effect caused by the lack of empathy as opposed to abundance. For to have compassion and empathy is acting as an expression of God. To do the opposite shows a disconnection to God Source. You are not less than others for being so, just a sheep who has strayed from the flock. We love you still and always will.

The act of compassion and empathy is a God-like thing to do and brings with it the joy of feeling Him around you and yes, within you. You open your mouth at times like this and the words of empathy come forth and lo and behold you have become an expression of God. We Angels observe that you have moments like this as well as moments where you don't and you believe God has left you. Nonsense Loved One. It is like a tap. You choose to turn it off when disbelief or lack of confidence overcome you and so you believe He has deserted you or that you are unworthy. All you have to do is turn the tap on and it will flow again freely as it did once before when you did have belief. You and you only can stop or restart the flow of love borne of the God source.

Do you think it too grand a concept to be directly in contact with God and the Angels? Do you feel it is only the position of priest or clergyman who can have that privilege? Have you been told you are not deserving and that God only talks to the aforementioned clergy? This is just a man-made belief designed to keep people in a position of being controlled. You know that. So why continue to allow this construct to control your life and destiny? You are more powerful than you know and because of this construct you become immobilised thinking it has ceased completely due to outside influences. We Angels so long for you to see that it is an illusion and that all it takes is to change how you perceive things. Once you have solved this problem then you are then free to be an expression of God. Be mindful you are never without God EVER!!

Be joyful in all things you do and in doing so a current will flow through you that can sustain you through all your trials. We come back to your little ones they do all that We have advised you to do automatically. It is like it is inbuilt. And yes We are glorifying them just as they deserve. One day they will be like you. And so We treat you with the same adoration. So if you are treated the same and loved the same as children that must mean you can be as they are too! An expression of God. For if you were to love yourself and others openly as they do, live in total joy of life as they do and live true to your life's purpose as they do, and fearlessly, then you are as they are. A true and pure form of an expression of God. Bless yourselves.

Children centre God within those who love them

(Phew! Here We go – Lisa) An extension of the statement We discussed above is that your young ones, in being an expression of God, can centre their elders. We sense in Lisa a dawning of recognition of this topic. At first she couldn't comprehend it because she was tired. A new day, a new view. A case in example We think. For her son centres her when he is around. He is a light being himself and is worthy of being mentioned. Lisa is embarrassed as she had no intention of him being included due to privacy. We mention him for her sake as well as to illustrate Our point. He is a wonderful, caring and well-meaning child and his face lights up at his mother's presence. He is still young enough to have a level of innocence and pure love in his heart. His mother feels this and feels glowing with pride (bear with Us Lisa). She feels buoyed by his love and feels a sense of purpose. She suddenly feels like she would fight to defend him tooth and nail. His presence in her life has given her strength and character she didn't know possible. Does this ring any bells? Yet look deeper. See what her son is doing to Our Lisa? He is making her actually BE herself. Who she truly is meant to be. A strong, confident, loyal and loving person. She is living true to herself, and to her nature. She can come out from behind her conditioning. He, wait for it, frees her. Frees her so she can be who God truly wants her to be. Yes, you guessed it! He centres God within her. For to be your true self is to be as God intended. To be God like. By this We mean as a pure expression of oneself, of God. Of the God energy within you all. Don't you see? You are all channels of Love. And what is God? LOVE!

You are worthy of this appointment. To say you are not to say God is unworthy. Remember you are expressions of God. We Angels are also another expression of God. Yes We are messengers of God and it doesn't mean you no longer need Us once you recognise He is working through you. Discovering He is within you is only the start of better things to come and We intend to be there all the way with you to share the journey and to learn from each other. I God's eyes no-one is greater than the other.

We Angels are not better than or of more value than man is. We simply have another role and that is to assist and protect. Of course there are many other tasks We have and We love the one where We look after you with great pride and reverence. Your little ones are also very Angel-like, hence the term you have which is 'Angelic'. They love unconditionally and feel everything you do with enormous hearts willing to fight for you and love you fiercely. They feel no fear because they haven't learnt that behaviour of 'belief system' yet. Don't get Us wrong. We don't mean to make you feel guilty or to blame for what you do for We know you are human and that is part of your growth. It is simply a tool through which you find your way back to God. Some of you get there quicker, others take a longer route. You are not judged as if in an Earthly classroom. You are simply made aware of the best way of accomplishing something as opposed to a way which will give you more grief. Why punish yourself? You make mistakes but it is you who judge each other. Not God. He does not judge you at all. And neither do your children. They are so young that they can remember what it is like to have God within them and how to use His loving energy to their benefit. This is the power of Love energy coursing through them. It carries them through troubled times and helps them to release things. This leads Us to mention 'Forgiveness'. For this is exactly what these loved ones are doing when they release with Love. In effect they are acting as you all should be. You are capable of this also.

We do not think of you any less when you don't. We simply exercise patience. For We know you will catch up. It is only a matter of time. We have faith in you always and smile at you when you fall but get up again anyway. For We see that you have learnt the meaning behind perseverance. It is God's will that you practice perseverance and stoicism. You are allowed to wonder over here and then over there emotionally in order to discover your completeness as long as you come back to your centre. That is the role of forgiveness! We bet you're surprised how We came back to that? To forgive is to release not just the other party, but to also bring you back to your centre. So you can move forward and not remain in suspended animation. Or to stay in the control of the other party's dynamic. To not forgive can cause you more harm than good and can stunt your growth towards being whole.

It takes a lot of effort, sometimes, to forgive another. You might be angry at being asked to forgive someone who has maligned you. Don't you think We Angels have your back? We are asking you to forgive for a reason. To not forgive is to simply press the pause button on your life and you will go no further. You can see where it is that you want to be but for some reason it just does not get any closer. Try as you might you remain stationary, and boy! Is it tiring. You slowly reach burnout and health issues start queuing up. You become grumpy and frazzled. Even a little angrier at those around you. But especially at yourself. This is no way to be Our Loved Ones. All this because you hold a grudge. It may be a deserved grudge you hold but, face it, it has the same effect on your progress like a lead balloon. We smile at Lisa's vernacular. She thinks We struggle with her vocabulary but it is adorable.

We digress. 'To forgive is Divine'. That is not a statement about class or worthiness. It just is simply 'divine'. That is what you feel when you realise how disabling the opposite is. Besides it also means you are getting closer to your divinity. Your God Source. Your centre. All this can be learnt by observing the little ones. See how quickly they forgive? All that matters to them is that you love them and they are willing to forego their own needs to put yours first by not arguing or being hurt. They release it quickly in order to instantly move forward, this if forgiveness. It transcends every other thing. It forces you to live in the now and not linger on what has been. To only look forward and to advance unhindered.

There is a saying that Lisa likes to use with her clients. Imagine you're a tightrope walker. You are balancing and you are slowly moving along the rope. Do you see where you want to be? Whatever you do don't look down! The moment you look down you set yourself up for failure immediately. You lose confidence and you wobble. The aim here is to not lose sight of your goal. Don't look down and keep moving towards your goal with absolute determination. Remember, perseverance and stoicism? The little ones don't want to remain static. They know it's healthy to proceed to their goals. They know not to linger on not forgiving. Not because of the pain associated with it but from the purity of their hearts and intentions. They have not always experienced pain yet and already they understand the concept of forgiveness. It is a tool they use in order to progress further along their path getting closer to their God.

If you allow, their very presence should ground you in reality not fantasy. They bring what is real home to you. Only NOW is what is important. What you did yesterday is gone. It doesn't interest them. Your sharing some space with a child will ground you in centredness. And that in itself should centre God within you.

THE INTUITIVE CHILD

Children are free spirits initially. They are usually care free. They are keenly aware of any stress their family may be experiencing and yet try t maintain equilibrium and joy. They're not being flippant. For they know that the only way forward is to step into joy. They choose joy as a way to recover. Let Us illustrate. A child may find his or her mother crying. It pains him to see her this way. For if she is unhappy then he is unhappy. Being unhappy is a heavy emotion. It weighs heavily on you slowing down healing. He knows this and knows the only way out of sadness is to rediscover joy. He brings her a flower from the garden and strokes her arm. He says sweet things to soothe her and tries to bring her attention to a drawing he had done earlier. Laughing while explaining to her what it is about. 'Look', he says, 'see the colours?'. His mother looks at the purple grass and the yellow sky in his painting. She looks into his sparkling, hope filled eyes and sees the depth of love he has for her and that his distracting her was his way of lightening her load. With hopes it will give her time to recover and resume her activities. It may appear a self-orientated act by the child but it is far from it. It is a selfless act and purely altruistic. If he is successful and gets praised he will grow and develop healthy problem solving skills. If chastised he ma retreat and start to question himself. Can you see the outcome We would prefer?

Try not to project your 'adult' perceptions onto your little ones. They are easily misunderstood this way and it causes them great pain indeed. It is because of laziness or extremely demanding jobs and lives that adults misunderstand their children. It is too much trouble to make the effort to bend down and look into their eyes to see what is truly being said. To see what they really meant and to explain to them reasons of theories of why things happen a certain way. Especially consequences and causes. If children are programmed from an early age to understand why and how things turn out a particular way and the consequences, if any, they will learn good, appropriate behaviours. If you know you have trained them well then any problems that arise should be easily explainable and dealt with better. If you don't do this and choose the easier option, projection, then you may be punishing these little ones for no reason and causing damage in the process. This is, tapping into her to sense her mood and then finding what God wants him to use to help her. He is dealing with the situation in a more intuitive way as opposed to cognitive. He is still using his cognitive processes but via his intuition. He 'feels' her pain in order to understand it and then process it to find the emotion to show her to draw her out of it. He is 'sensing' first and foremost. He can access his empathy and problem solving skills (emotional and mental schemas – Lisa) via his intuitive barometer.

Believe it or not this is what you are designed to do but most just rely on the cognitive of emotions alone. This is akin to you riding a unicycle when it is much easier to ride a three wheeler which stays more balanced with less effort. Again Lisa, why do you resist Us? (you can see I am struggling with accepting what is being said – Lisa) Trust that the message will reach its mark. Lisa thinks it's a strange analogy We give you and so her cognitive kicks in to analyse it instead of her trusted intuition. Ha! Another example for you. Our beloved Lisa is on her unicycle! (haha – Lisa). We put to her that have We led her astray yet? (No – Lisa) Then, as an example, Lisa should trust Us but using her intuition to tune into Us. We sense in her that this is akin to sharing Our energy. This way she can 'read' Us instead of second guessing what We are about to say. Or SHOULD say. We can take care of that Ourselves. If you are using your intuition then you will be totally trusting Us with what is to come. You will be living, as they say, in the 'now'.

It is also like being blindfolded and falling into Our arms with absolute faith We well catch you. Lisa is laughing now as We show her the next analogy. Imagine there is a remote control, just like the television one, for you. However there are only three visible buttons. Two black ones and one red one. The black one on the left is the 'cognitive' button and the black one on the right is the 'emotive' one. Press either one and you can focus on either of these attributes solely. However there is one problem. You can only concentrate on one attribute at a time. Why can't all three work together? This is why We have believers and sceptics. One is one extreme and the other another extreme. It takes skill to work all three aspects of your make up together to find a balance and connection to the others. Such as a sceptic. He is too reliant on the cognitive and so has lost contact with his intuitive aspect. He thinks he is astute but We see him as hindered in his so called 'objectivity'. Imagine, if you will, that We are your personal trainers. You juggle each 'button', being one way (emotional) then the other (psychological) and occasionally dip into intuitive. You tell Us that you can't possibly do all three at once! However it is like a muscle, We say, and all it takes is stamina and dexterity. 'But we can't do it' you say. Oh yes you can, We say. It just takes practice and effort. Yes, effort. That's a tough one We hear you say. 'Hup – two – three – four!'. Really, Lisa, We wish you would stop giggling. See? We Angels DO have a sense of fun. Despite what some might say.

We have to use humour sometimes to make a point. After all We Angels revel in the energy you create when you laugh. That energy is vibrant, jubilant, energising joy. It lifts you to a higher level of sensation. The energy is very Angelic. Because it is a lighter energy and one that is totally uplifting for you. Most advisable state to be in don't you think? The kind of energy that can make effort a whole lot easier, hmmm? So the moral of the story? Use humour and good spirits (pun intended) to make the act of balancing all three a lot easier. We are talking about you. Our children, being intuitive. When you truly are being yourself it is easier to access your intuition. You can then analyse it from the other two perspectives. You can intellectualise it to understand it and pick it apart before putting it back together again. You can feel your way to it and enjoy the capacity it gives you. They are intrinsically joined. Again Lisa struggles with words and tries to correct Us. She relented and went back to what We originally told her. THAT, Our Loved Ones, is listening to your intuition.

Getting back to children. As We have said you are all children of God. However We refer now to your little ones. Those smaller versions of you. They are here to teach you not necessarily the other way around. They live as you should live, carefree and lovingly. Lovingly not just to others but also to themselves. To teach them it is not hard to juggle the triple effect We discussed earlier. They see the common sense. The common sense in its existence. These little loved ones are pure and untainted and live as best as only they know how. Some of you may think We are discussing a metaphysical way of being intuitive. This does occur and surely exists, but We refer here to how they live. We do talk to your children and sometimes they see Us. They also see other helpers in spirit as well as loved ones who have passed over. This, We have just informed Lisa, is yet another book to fill (ooooooer – Lisa). But for now We are simply talking about how you (your children) are made up. Intuition has many aspects as We have illustrated. Children are naturally psychic and see spirit very easily. They are energetically open to all forces and so need protecting. The most important way is to maintain a good level of common sense and open mindedness. To tell them right from wrong. Up from down. And to use that all important tool – love. To use love in everything they do will ensure that at least they are doing the job effectively. They channel Our energy so much easier than most adults. Not because you adults are less than. But because most of you have learnt to block that 'knowing energy' and rely purely on what you see not what you feel. This is ok but it limits you. These two aspects are meant to be used in unison hence that statement how sceptics limit their view. They rely on the intellect alone. Sometimes man becomes too reliant on that one 'button' – intellect.

You have a saying, 'Everything in moderation'. Intellect has it's place and is crucial for survival. If used too much it can blinker you. So use it wisely. This is what children do naturally. They are extremely sensitive little machines and soak up all sorts of information. Not just with their intellect, but with their emotions and, you guessed it, their intuition. We rest Our case.

What these children need from you and from God

What do you need? A home to live in, food to sustain you, clothing for warmth and protection, electricity and water to run your home, family and loved ones for support. If you're lucky a car for transport. All of these things can be called 'basics'. You need all of the above just to exist on a day to day basis and without them, especially if that is all you've known, you may struggle. Of course We know there are some of you who do have less than this. How do they survive? They live day by day possibly begging and scrimping for money to buy their food. They sometimes have family. At least the surviving members as some may have passed due to malnutrition or illness that would normally be treatable if only they had the finances or even access to medical services. However they push on. They have to as they have no choice. Sometimes they are sad but life still has to be lived. What keeps them alive? In some cases it is faith. Not always to a God. Although many times it is. Sometimes they are so poor and without possessions that there is only hope and faith left. That is what keeps them going, possibly the only thing that does. God does not mind how you show faith. Just so long as you know that you can use it. Yes, that's right, 'use' it.

You see faith has a purpose and that is to create focus. Focus on a goals. In this case that goal is purely survival. Faith is a tool given by God to help you live moment to moment whilst staying (knowingly or not) connected to Him. You see, He doesn't mind if you are aware of Him or not because He has faith in YOU! Faith that you will find your way back home to Him. No matter how you do it. It's not a matter of 'if' as it is 'when'. He isn't going anywhere. He wants you to feel what faith is like and helps you to create life lessons which lead to finding the faith you need to go on.

Children do this naturally without urging. It's innate in them. They don't always know it consciously. But they just know that to have faith means a healthy expectancy and trust in the essential good within man. And of course, in God.

They sometimes have no other choice if they are in situations that have the ability to cause distress. Such as abuse or poverty and illness. They know that in order to cope they HAVE to have faith in a higher power. This is not false hope of delusion. It is the higher divine aspect of themselves which knows that God exists and that We will provide for you regardless. Especially His support. Many poor people have their own local churches that they attend. They have found a way to cope by actually physically turning to God. Well, not just physically, but the churches and temples are a physical representation of God and their physical bodies attend as does their mind, spirit and soul. They go with love and commitment to nourishing their souls with the support that is there. The commonality and familiarity. To find others of the same ilk. Same outlooks and life experiences. To also create a familial network where children of these people have extended family and other 'siblings' as role models. This creates stability that may be lacking in other areas such as poverty. Family values are upheld and traditions are born. Laughter and love can be expressed easily in this close knit community like situation. All essential things to help you to keep on keeping on.

Your children need this from you. If you want to ensure that your children grow up feeling secure then you need to create an environment that is conducive to that. You may do it through religion. You may do it through clubs and sports. The essential thing is to show your children how to maintain that faith that they are born with. For if they see you become jaded and cynical then they lose their faith and look at things as they seem through YOUR eyes. They eventually take on your point of view. If you are down, they ae down. If you give up, then the risk of them seeing you model that type of behaviour and it changing them is greater. They need consistency from you as well as strength. You need to guide them as they learn new skills. To be patient when they fudge it and have to start over again. To smile at what they achieve regardless of what level they get to. Also importantly, to NOT project your insecurities and worries onto them. Allow yourself to revel in their innocence and joy of life for THEY can re-educate you. We say re-educate as opposed to teach because We don't wish to patronise you and assume that you are not learned yourself.

We appreciate your ability to excel in you own life and that you do work hard to strive towards the best for all in your family. Lisa fears We are a little hard on you all. Not al all. We love you so, so much and sing your praises as often as We can. We whisper it in your ears when you are losing faith and doubt yourself and even doubt God and Us. We help your guides to bring wonderful news and life events for you to enjoy and celebrate. This book is meant to be constructive and to assist you in seeing light from dark. Sometimes you have to see the shadow in order to understand the light source (ie. Your problems and your achievements). We hope you find understanding and validation within these pages.

Potential problems are highlighted because you can learn through Our analogies a more effective way of living and of being a good example to your little ones. Please not We Angels do not see you as faulted or that what you do as mistakes. You need to hear positive things from Us and mostly from God. We ARE messengers of God and have a responsibility to you and your children. So We try to paint a picture what is working and what won't and how to get back on track. That is if you feel you have lost your way. We do not assume you have done so. This is merely objective suggestion.

Your children need you to listen to Us as it indirectly affects them. They also need God this way too. He is always there to listen to them and without being critical or judgemental. Children already have everything they need within them. It is only over time that it becomes more distant from their day to day functioning. You see, it never actually leaves you as you leave childhood and enter adulthood. It is simply like a cluttered attic inside of you and the connection to God is like a manuscript that has been mislaid in this attic. It never goes away. It's just tucked in some dusty corner waiting to be rediscovered. All you need is to go looking for it and pick up where you left off as a trusting and loving child. Don't feel that to be trusting and loving is leaving you vulnerable and wide open to inappropriate actions.

See, We are with you always and all you have to do is call on Us and We shall be there. As a feeling of love and knowing within your heart. You see to call on Us does not necessarily mean you will hear harps and choral music and then glowing visions of winged beings. Although We have been called upon to show ourselves this way before. Usually We are the voice of reason within you and that warm glow in your heart which tells you that you are loved. This gives you confidence to step forward as it makes you feel supported from within. It is how We work. We work WITH you. Once you recognise We work then there is no stopping you from accessing Us and Our energy any time you need to. As Lisa says, its like a muscle. The more you work it, the more effective it becomes. Now We get to the exciting part. To do what We have just suggested lets Us Angels into your heart and of course We are messengers of God. So to let Us enter your energy field and your heart is actually letting God in. Aren't We clever? Children need to do this and naturally do it. You, as adults, tend to train them to redirect this urge into the religions you have created. So the methods these children now use are contaminating the natural and innate abilities to call on God. Religion has it's place and is essentially well meant but can be a bit misguided.

What children really want is just God and His untampered with purity and glow. They don't need the complicated constructs that adults have made. The little ones method is much easier to access and portable too. They don't need great stone monuments carved over decades and dedicated to a deity. They just go within and talk to Him. They want Him NOW and intuitively connect to Him immediately. Not that We say intuitively. To go to church is to go to god physically. That is great! However really He is inside all of you and goes wherever you go and you could say God is in your pocket. (Tut tut Lisa. Do compose yourself). This is all that your children want from God. Easy accessibility and consistent support by which they feel when they sense His energy around and inside them. He is known quantity to them and they know they can talk to Him anytime they need to and without judgement. Children are easy to please and they know fake from real. Also, because they are naturally intuitive, they used it more often to soothe themselves. You, or rather most of you, have lost contact with this ability and have been conditioned to believe it doesn't exist no matter, We know one day you will. We look forward to that day and will greet you with open arms. As will your children.

The future for these children

Cares are a reasonably new invention. A century or so old admittedly, but nevertheless new in the grand scheme of things. However, since they have been invented, life has been made easier and at the same time more risky. A hundred years or so ago man did not live with cars as you do now and them then it was but a dream. A fantasy, and something to come. Back then they looked forward with their imaginations thinking about wonderful and amazing inventions which seem like a lifetime away. Their imaginations were captivated and they dreamt of one day flying too. What is it in these people that kept them going until one day these dreams were actualised? Hope. Hope is what man has when he looks to the future. Hope sustains you. Hope makes you optimistic and most importantly it keeps you moving and looking forwards. Nothing weighs you down more than looking back to your past. It can be like a dead weight. Completely slowing you down and stopping your progression. Admittedly reviewing life events past can help shape a better future as long as you do so constructively. However to remain there mourning what could have been is so damaging for your soul and railroads you off your life path. It also takes you away from Us. Or seemingly so. You will feel trapped and inert. No motivational energy at all. And this will go on feeding it day after day and will keep you at a stuck point. Stuck in the past. That is exactly what this chapter is for. To help you see that looking ahead is the only way to go, not looking back. To forgive is also to release yourself so as to be able to look and move forward.

As We have mentioned before children already have this ability. They release things because they know that to retain them keeps the negative feelings within them. The pain too. We are hoping that by getting Lisa to write this book that We will reach as many of you as possible and in so doing affect positively the lives of future generations of children.

Bit and small. We aim to assist, not hinder and have complete joy in communicating with you. We often talk to your little ones and they to Us. They feel Our energy around them as feelings of love and happiness. Contentedness and compassion for others. It is so because in children it is closer to the surface. It is in all of you but metaphorical 'boxes' of information in the 'attic' have covered it. A lot of you have worked hard to recover it from the depths and to maintain it. It is not your fault at all. Life, as they say, just gets in the way. You are by no means less than these little ones. You are one and the same.

We just want to realise and recognise it in yourselves by Our illustrating situations to you. All that We have brought up is what just makes you, you. It doesn't darken Our perceptions of you. It simply adds to the colourfulness of which is yourself. It's not good or bad, light or dark, right or wrong. It is ALL essential in making you who you are. Even the problems (not mistakes) you encounter. It is all an aspect of you which is a good thing for it highlights the rich tapestry that is your character. Your personality. Your being. Lisa wanted to write soul but We stopped her for your soul is perfect and doesn't need attention. Your soul is what you originate from. It is what is closest to God. An aspect of God, if you will. It is the part of you that always will be around. It is eternal and is tapped into the eternal love of God. It is where your energy comes from. From a point of eternal love. It is where your intentions come from. It is also where you are heading. You being the children of God. For this book is about your little ones as they are children but so are you, yourself. Your future, whether you are aware of it or not, is with God. You will return to Him one day. We will welcome you with open arms. The wisdom of children is there for all to use and as they grow towards their future they learn things from within as well as from without. We do not want to talk about war or global issues in this book. That is not the future We are talking about. The future We talk about is enlightenment. You are heading towards enlightenment and it doesn't matter which route you take, be it the long intricate route or the quick route. You will return to God. THAT is your future and that of your little ones. It doesn't matter whether you believe in Him or not. That belief system is only a temporary outer cover to cater to your needs in this lifetime. Yes We said 'this lifetime'. You do, as they say, experience many lifetimes. For if you are a non-believer this lifetime does not prove anything because you will soon meet Him when your time comes anyway. What a joyous experience that will be for all concerned! We say this lovingly. You may need to have the experience of scepticism this lifetime in order to feel the rapture when you finally do meet Him and Us, of course.

Acceptance of God and His Children

What is acceptance? It is releasement. We laugh as Lisa is looking through a dictionary. It does not matter, child. We have created a word. It is akin to forgiveness. Except in a different context. Acceptance is not passivity or complacency. It is releasing all preconceived expectations. Acceptance frees you as does forgiveness. Acceptance shows you have learnt the lessons. You have learnt your lessons and are now ready to move on. In turn it then lets in the new and purges the old. Why stay locked into the past and with old, stale ways of living that, quite frankly, do not work anymore? Lisa is pausing here. We think this resonates with her at this point in time. You see she is at a cross roads in her life and she has to release the old in order to accept the new. She's been prolonging it for so long now due to resistance and procrastination and right now feels like she is being lectured to. We love her so much and see that she struggles with her issues that have been with her since childhood. She is vulnerable and frightened sometimes as are you. Yet other times We remind her of her strengths. For when you are in that space of strength it, in turn, creates, or rather, makes way for easier transition into acceptance. Its only when you are fearful and feeling defeated that it becomes harder to accept things. You instead cling to what you know and daren't step out onto that ledge. After all it takes a leap of faith to jump from the ledge in order to see if you can fly.

We find it strange that you little ones are forever flying around and taking those leaps of faith. They don't even give it a second thought. Off they go running around and then leaping. Just knowing (how DO they know?) that they'll be caught. For it's the act of leaping that is the whole point. 'Why put off till tomorrow what you can do today?' that saying of yours goes. Stubbornness. Procrastination. Resistance.

Resistance, fear, doubt. These things all hamper your ability to just take action. To just leap. 'Nothing ventured, nothing gained' is another saying of yours. Some of you see it as foolhardy and naïve. Take a look again. Is it really? Or is it the only way to live? Lisa has a saying that We think is very apt. 'There is naïve trust, then there is wise trust'. If you engage wisdom before you leap, better still live with wisdom as a way of life, then you will be prepared at all times. You won't be jumping blindly. Even the shyest of squirrels needs to reach for an acorn from outside of his comfort zone. He has to creep out of his burrow some time to eat and brave the world outside. Some things are done out of necessity, yet some can be done…..because they can be done. You ask too many questions. This in itself shows your lack of trust in Us. Your lack of trust in yourselves! Your little ones just trust and come from a place of love and joy. They are uncensored. Uninhibited. They are living fully as God intended and thoroughly enjoying it. Yes, they sometimes fall down or get into scrapes. However they themselves know the healthiest thing to do is to get right back up and try again. It's only your conditioning that inhibits them and causes them to pause and then get caught up in 'failure'. When, quite naturally, they are ready and able to just simply 'accept' in order to move forward.

Our message to you is 'why can't you just accept?'. It is the only way to release yourself in order to progress. Lack of trust shows you haven't accepted the status quo. You can, believe it or not, do this wisely not naively. Accept but with open eyes and an open heart. You don't have to be a victim of sorts. Haplessly trusting and then tripping and blaming Us or God for the tumble. Take your life firmly in your hands and steer it over the precipice. Plan where you want to land and allow a little freefall. Flow with the breeze as you glide gracefully to the terrain below. Awareness is the key and to have awareness and being very present in the 'now' will assist you to control the direction of your own life. Have a say in where you want to go. Not just with others but with yourself also. For YOU have to believe you have the authority to do so yourself. It is a fine balance between control and trust. You people can get a little lazy and just do one of these things at a time which, inevitably, sets you up for failure and ultimately disappointment. Not to mention negative association and obsession.

We merely remind you of this and do not judge you for it. We Angels want you to realise your full potential and in order to do this We work through Lisa to describe to you the things that hold you back. Lisa is also learning as We talk and has been forced to see things she had been putting off from seeing. She sometimes fights herself regarding typing what We have spoken to her. We urge her strongly to go ahead and write anyway and then afterwards she does indeed read it back to herself and finally understands where We are coming from. A place of love. We Angels fully accept reality which is why We can be so brutally honest sometimes. For the only way through it is to accept. If you don't accept things then you become stuck and sometimes that can be in a place of pain. Do you really want that Loved Ones? We certainly don't. It causes Us great angst to see you stunt your own growth through stubbornness and fear. And BOY!! Are you stubborn! Not only do you refuse to listen to Our warnings and whispers, but you also refuse to take responsibility when it all goes pear shaped (as Lisa would say. Yes, Lisa, We are indeed quoting you!). See how Lisa doesn't accept her own wisdom? She also doesn't like being used as an example. Fear of sounding arrogant and self-absorbed. So many constraints you Loved Ones have on yourselves. How else is God's word going to be heard but through your own lips? Again We use the word 'accept'. Accept that you are God's children and that all that comes from your lips really has its origins in God. After all, He is all who is and all who will ever be, whether it be through you or some other being. You need to accept this. Accept the Lord, your God. In all ways that He exists. All forms and expressions.

Blessings
Gabriel

LAST WORDS

Although this book was written in 2006 When my son was only 12 I wrote it in two weeks and after my first book 'Wisdom of Love – Words from Gabriel'. Both were written in a space of about two months. I set here today in April 2012 having finished retyping them out due to a glitch on the floppy disc and finding a lot of amendments and also understandings. I see now I was destined to reread it as it helped me even now. My beautiful son, who is the light of my life, is now six foot and eighteen. He has been my teacher and my twin flame. He is the other half of my whole being. If it weren't for him I would not be doing what I am doing and being successful at it. It has been a journey where the child in my life has helped me become a successful psychic on a very successful and renowned psychic line. I have worked hard to get here but it is all because of this wise beautiful soul in my son who has helped me on this journey. I hope this book helps you as it has myself.

I have also finished the third book in this trilogy 'Wisdom of Time – Words from Gabriel' this year. So even though there is about six years in difference between them I hope they still carry over in the theme of guidance from Gabriel. Gabriel is someone I now work closely with and channel Him. I see Gabriel as a Him even though some may see Him as a Her. Neither are wrong yet I relate to 'Him' as a he for ease of writing this book. The energy is the same and 'He' is still beautiful. I leave you now and hope that you get pleasure out of these books. Look out for further books as I have many ideas flowing through me now.

Blessings
Lisa

Wisdom of Time – Words from Gabriel

Introduction

Hello there again! It's been about five years since my first book and am only now at time of writing (8th May 2011) had time to sit down and start this third instalment. My life has taken on a huge transformation since that time and I am incredibly in my own business. I kept getting told to write this book but kept postponing it due to other commitments. But spirit has a way of persuading us sometimes. It's a lazy Sunday and in particular Mother's Day. I am sitting on my bed, the hub of the house, with my now six foot, seventeen year old son lying across the end of it where he usually sits only now his legs hang over the edge. He was twelve years old when I wrote the first book and second book, and now is almost a man. He has been my inspiration for all that I do inn spiritual practice and is the reason why I am practicing it in the first place.

I still have my animals, the three cats: Rameses, Rosie and Casper and the budgie Lizzie (who swears like a trouper) and when I have one on one readings I have to remover her because she is so noisy and rude. Lord knows if a readings is taped by a client that there's colourful language coming from the background I will be red faced. The dog is still here and is now twelve years old and deaf as a doorpost. We have gained a new family member, a goldfish called Tiger but nick name is Bloop due to him constantly blooping at me when I go near the tank in hopes of getting fed.

I work in my business of sometimes domestic cleaning and working on the psychic phone lines as a psychic medium. I am also looking to getting more belly-dance classes up and running in the not too distant future.

All of this is where I am right now and is a demonstration of the 'Time' that has passed since last we met. Which brings me to the title of this book. The title was illusive at first, but the something happened to bring it to mind instantaneously. My beloved father in law passed away. Seeing my son, his father and my mother in law and sister in law all grieving and my realisation that the three generations spanned across time. That we all go through significant phases in our lives and each generation represents a particular stage in life. We can see our future in our elders and our past in our little ones. Acceptance of our fate is important and yet embraced because life does go on, in one form or another. We go on. Our souls, at least do. Our souls are timeless, ageless, eternal and always flawless. As that saying goes 'We are spiritual beings having a spiritual experience.' Time is one thing we as humans try to out run. We watch our clocks. We time our eggs (haha). Spirit, on the other hand, have a different take on time as Gabriel will no doubt mention shortly. There is a lot to be learnt but yet we have achieved so much in our own school of life.

I have found that I have had to manage my time better. My son is growing so big so fast and there is no way I can stop that so I can keep the cherubic young thing he once was. He now is taller than me and broad like a true man and training for an apprenticeship. He is individuated from me and doesn't need 'mothering'. Although he does really. So even he has a struggle with time overlaps. Being a man child, not quite a man yet not quite a child. He wants the respect of an adult, as we all did at that ae, but still to know there is security and comfort at home. At least until he can create it himself. I step back and try to let go of controlling this 'time' in our lives. I watch in awe the creation of my life flowing on into his life and one day into the lives of his children. He is fine. I a have done my job. He is now in the time of his life and in his prime. I can witness how with time comes experience and wisdom which can only be gained through time worn living of life.

It's been five months since starting this book now and I have been busy in my business and my study not to mention with teaching belly-dance and now establishing a curriculum for teaching psychic development. I must have needed, pardon the pun, time……to make time to just focus on this book. I have had such an intensive year with a lot of demands asked of me. My son is still seventeen and is still working towards an apprenticeship and I have seen precious little of him as he lives with his father now. But when we do see each other time melts away and I realise we adore each other. I mention this because time is important. Or rather the marking of time is important. We observe the marking of time to identify specific occurrences and milestones in our life. I can look back since I have first started this introduction to see how I have grown and evolved and am proud of myself that I am learning my lessons quicker. Before time would drag and I would resist my growth as I was tired and impatient. Now I have rested and taken 'time' to invest to myself. I feel so much more present in the time as it is now. Time has many layers. It's where we have been, where we are and where we are going. It's what we set aside to do something. I have just not had the time to do this and now I have a little gap in my study year I have decided to live up to my promise to Arch Angel Gabriel. He is with me now and I can smell freesias, my favourite flower. This is a sign that the Angels are with me. I have put on my dvd of The Nanny on in the background to keep the atmosphere light and jovial. I love laughter and to me the sense of the funny and amusing makes the time pass quicker or more happier. I have my cats all sitting on the bed watching me and keeping me company. This time in my life is fulfilling and I want to help others to feel fulfilment.

I, by no means, assume time to come won't be challenging and testing. However I line in the now. Which, by the way, is still a part of time. It's the moment we are in that we are momentarily aware of. Memory keeps us busy weighing up the past in order to predict the future. I hope my books are entertaining and enlightening. I love working with the Arch Angels and Angels. These books are not my idea but 'Theirs'. I have no say in this and willingly contribute by being Their instrument. Please feel free to email me at lisa@lisahodgson.com.au. I welcome communication and contributions toward feedback. We are a family on this planet and today it's a small world. In no time you can make friends across the country and the world. I shall leave you in Gabriel's capable hands and see you on the other side of this book in the conclusion.

God bless and blessed be. Lisa xxx

Wisdom of Time – Words from Gabriel

Hello Love Ones. I am delighted to see you again and to have this chance to talk to you once more! Lisa is ready now to let me work through her. This is the 'time'. The lesson for her was the importance of managing her time and allocating some time for Us to work through her. We smile as We see her learn her lessons and realise she is capable, more capable than she first thought. She has willingly let Us have some of her precious 'time' in order for Us to talk. We respect her time because she is hard working, diligent soul who has only ever wanted to help others. We did not want to get in the way of this important job Lisa has. We mean that. It is truly important. Others benefit from her role. All of you are deeply loved and respected. Your lives are all measured in moments and each moment is as important as the next. It's these moments which instil in you the knowledge that God is working through you. The moments you become aware of the times which are significant are the moments which shows a snapshot of your lives which demonstrates your use of time or your lesson in that time. Time is fleeting. It comes and it goes. It runs past you in a constant stream like the film in a tape it rolls and rolls and keeps going, never stopping but each moment is still full. Positively pregnant with essence and energy which stays with you as you go through and navigate in time. Trying to capture Time is akin to catching sunlight in a bottle. Loved ones you exist in time whether you measure it or not. Time may be seen as a destination. It is seen as a guide as to what and how you are shaped. Time in the future is a manifestation of the act of Hope. Hope lives seemingly in the future. You, my Loved Ones, need Hope. It is an essential. Hoe drives you forward. It creates momentum and motivation. It gives you Our Loved Ones a reason to live god's life which he created in you. He has given you life. In this life He has given you time to life it. Not a finite time as you, Our Loved Ones, are infinite and never ceasing to exist. You live in awareness of the moment. In fact We encourage living in the moment. This is because to not do so cause you, Our Children, pain.

Regret, shame, guilt, anxiety, hate, anger, resentment, fear and distrust all stem from Your losing sight of living in the moment. Living for the future completely puts your life on hold Loved Ones. You stop hearing Gods whispers and you cease to listen to your hearts desires. You desire what is not yet to be instead of enjoying what there is in the now. Creation is in the 'now' not the future. The only important moment is now. However We in spirit are aware that Our Loved Ones on Earth need to be aware of the future based on the fact you, dear beautiful souls, have measured time, past, present and future. This is in order to gauge and be prepared for expected events, or to measure your intended actions based on past actions in order to be wise and careful. This is understandable. Nothing that you do is wrong. It is merely We in spirit dear Loved Ones, wish to help enlighten you as to how to alleviate your anxieties.

The Past

The past, dear Loved Ones, is what has been. It is a record of where you have come from and is a reminder of why you are here and where you are going. This is simple We know. However the past is nonetheless important to you. To Us Angels We exist in no time. We see all as it is past, present and future and are timeless. We see where you once were as We were there with you whispering in your ear. We see that you do now and finally We see what is to come. We live across time and within the spiritual realm where there is no measurement. We do not live according to a measurement. We exist outside of time. At least as you know to be.

You, Our Loved Ones, are also timeless beings who live on through time and across eons. You may shed your outer casing and take on new forms but the inner you is eternal and made up of your Creator's energy. You come from God and you will return to God. God runs through you and is you. God is a benevolent and loving Father who loves you dearly and you can take on His love like a mantle to protect yet nourish you. God Himself straddles your so called time and oversees all motions created in time to establish a history to your peoples. God is Love and Love is eternal. Never ending. Ongoing. Endless. Immortal. Essential. All of love is flowing through life on Earth and is the cause of your creation. God is your Creator and works with Love to mould and create love in its manifest form. You. Love is eternal. Love is endless. Love is timeless. Love runs eternally through time and is the fuel, the energy that runs life. So as you see Love exists at all times. Past, present and future. Love has always been here and will still be here in times to come.

Love is the currency which is used to navigate time. To plug into time you need to be using and aware of where Love is in your life. You cannot go into the future whole unless you utilise Love to fuel and guide you. The past reminds you of what Love has gotten for you. If your memories are negative then the experiences did not reflect true Love. Love is a source of joy and creation not an act of betrayal and deceit. When you look to the past and see what worked for you and what worked against you and you will see that Love is pure and clear in its motives. Having said that We want to convey that ironically Love even is involved in the negative too. Only in the sense that Love is teaching you lessons. Love is there all the time to rescue you or to help you. Looking back at your past helps you to grow forward. Helps you to remember that which serves you and that which doesn't. The past has a lot of Hope in it. You will see where you had hope and where that hope was well founded. You see the lessons where hope was misguided. You see that you are ok with that because you can see where you had lessons and that you also may have felt your intuition. Seeing how you listened to your intuition and heeded it and found you were on the right path is enlightening. It's what God wants you to do. To see the spiritual lessons in the past. To look back and smile to yourself about how perceptive you were and how misguided. All is still good, though. You see why now. You are safe now. You see that despite life's travails you are still in one piece. You are a survivor. Keep going. To go into the future you have to be at peace about the past.

To live in intuitiveness you are to be living across time and with time. You would be working with time and not against it. We do not mean you are less for not doing so. We mean we want you to be aware you are doing it. In being aware of such things means that you are letting go of the measurement of time and not limiting your scope by doing so. To measure time is to limit time. To limit yourself and your experience of time. Living across time is more advisable and this is done by letting go of the past and not attempting to control the future. The past describes who you are. When people ask you about your accomplishments what they are asking you is where have you come from and what have you done to get where you are? Not in those words but by asking about you. What made you who you are now? You are a product of your so called past. You came forward through time to the present through the experiences you had then and have records of such. Your resume, your photo album, you certificates. All symbols of where you have come and what you have accomplished on that path. Nothing in the past is wasted. Never should you regret what has once been. All of it made you who you are today Loved Ones. You are marvellous, beautiful beings with souls given directly from your creator. He has moulded you. He has created that little spark that is within you and directs you to act out the life He has given you in the best way you know how. He takes great joy in seeing your inventiveness and creativity and has raptures when you meet your mark. He truly is your Father and loves you as such. You are His children and He loves you dearly.

Everything you do is an extension of Him and His gloriousness. So where you have come from and what you did back then was purely an expression of Him and His existence in your life. Everything you did in your past He says to you "Look at where you were. Look at where you are. Look at where you are going. Blessings upon you child. You are all that you need. You and I are one".

Nothing can be gained by calling the past back. Nothing can be gained by mourning the past. Wanting what was in the past now is wanting to control time. This is impossible. Time is a gift for you to deal with your lessons. Have you noticed how sometimes time flies and sometimes it drags? This is because you harness time and use it to propel you forward. Or when it drags you try to control it and believe it or not, stop it. When you want time to stop because you are not happy you notice time dragging. This is not harnessing it but holding it down like holding down a helium filled balloon. You cannot control the past and you cannot bring it back. You need to deal with the now, which We will talk about soon.

The past is important. We want to make that clear. The past is something which is maintained by your beautiful selves. You were gifted with hindsight and memory. We in spirit do not at all want you to stop having memories. We see the benefits in reflection and remembrance. Remembrance is important in honouring those whom you love and who have passed. Remembrance brings the past into the present in order for you to learn your lessons in order to go into the future with wisdom and awareness. Awareness is why you are here Dear Ones. Awareness can only be brought about over time. Awareness is with you from the very beginning until the very end. It transcends time. It, however, is with you from when you were born. In the past so to speak. As a newborn you become aware. Your first awareness would have been the coldness of the air as you entered the world from your mother's womb. Awareness of the smell of your mother's milk. Awareness of noises and sensations. This awareness is there for you to take into the future. It is what you use to program yourself and build your coping mechanisms and drives from. To help you prepare for what life may bring you.

As you can see your past is integral as to who you are and how you arrived at where you may be now. One thing is for sure Loved One, Love existed then and it exists now. Love is the current which runs all the way through time and on into the future. We shall explore this shortly but to finish on the topic of the past We shall conclude with our discussion on the past with Our advice to you on reflecting on it. The past is a gift to you. You may find yourself looking back and being grateful for the lessons you were given and grateful for surviving tough times as well as gratitude for the positive and happy times. You had to go through it and at the time it was you present but it is now you past. Be proud of yourselves for you have weathered great storms and balanced between great highs and lows. The past is the origins of your beginning to realise all that exists is Love. Love is where the fuel that makes the world go around and moves you through time to get to your ultimate destination.

Present

Hello Love One! Nice to meet you here in the 'Present'! There is nothing strange about this. For the present is where you have always been. This is the most important aspect of time. Time is suspended in the present. It is impossible to measure the present……nor would We want you to. The present is where time does not move nor does it lag. If you are truly in the present and in the moment you will feel a suspended type of feeling. As if you are just existing in the moment. A feeling of suspension and floating. Total awareness of this actual moment and awareness of who you are, a child of God. Believe it or not you can meet God in the present. This is why many get lost and disillusioned. Because they are too focussed on what has been and what is yet to come. They do not realise that by doing that they have lost their way. They have lost their connection to God. It's ok. God hasn't gone anywhere. God is here in the present. God is found in the present, hence why when you are aware of being in the present and feel a glow of centredness means you are with God in that moment. How addictive is that? To know that God has never left you and yet is even waiting for you now in the present! Is this not amazing? To know that that is how easy it is to find Him and be with Him. It is like the image of a rollercoaster. You have to stay in your centre in order to remain safely within the cart on the rollercoaster. If you were to lean outward from the cart you would feel your centre of gravity slip and a strong pull away from your centre. God is sitting next to you in the cart and He reaches across to grab your sleeve and pull you back in to centre and safely centred in the cart again. This is the feeling God wants you to feel in order to know how to find your centre again within this very moment. He is there with you every step but if you lean away from Him His voice becomes fainter but still exists nonetheless. All you have to do is lean back towards Him in order to hear Him clearly again. It's like going in and out of focus. He is always and forever still there but you can sometimes make Him seem out of focus or in focus. It's finding that happy medium where you lean towards Him the more you hear Him. Being stuck in the past makes you lean away from His voice. You are not in the truth. For the truth only exists in the now. To truly hear God you need to be in the present and be available to work with Him in the now because He does His best work in the present. And for you to be a part of this miracle you need to be here in the present to experience it with Him…..and Us. Life is meant to be lived and the present is where life is most colourful and giving with experiences. You miss so much when obsessing about the future.

We hear you ask 'when will I meet Mr/Miss Right?' or 'when will I get more money?'/ These perceptions are future focussed and you won't get any answers because the future is not yet created. What you have to realise is you have all the power to create that future you so desire. In accordance with the power of manifestation you all love to talk about dear Loved Ones, you are more than capable of manifesting what you desire but choosing it in the present. For everything begins in the present. All decisions are made in the present and all projects ae kicked off from the present. Each thought. Each belief. Each concept and each desire is felt only in the now. Surely you do have memories of feelings, decisions and desires which in and of itself indicates that they existed in the past. However back then that was your present. To have your memory is a gift from God. It was something which gives you the instincts you have. Instincts have an impulse type quality and are a fleeting connection between perceiving what's occurring in the now and what you have already experienced in order to weigh up the level of danger or safety. Instincts are important and help you survive hazardous situations or lead you to places of safety or sustenance. It was more acutely sensed in your ancestors and yet you still have that ability just faintly whispering to you and leading you to where it is best for you. Having intuition is akin to instincts. In fact it is closely related and is used in tandem with instincts. Intuition is the heightened level of instinct which is a sense of something which cannot be perceived by the five normal senses. It has been commonly seen in animals in the wild. The heightened instincts which comes from their connection to intuition. With senses of smell and sight which are also heightened animals can tune into a herd mentality and also do amazing things which humans cannot at this stage.

We, Loved Ones, bring to your attention the concept of intuition because it illustrates how you can tune into your intuition in order to live in the moment yet in the same time transcend time. Past, present and future. When living your normal lives you move through life head down and moving sometimes by rote. When, We wonder, will you turn your face up to God/ You fleetingly dip in when confronted with distressing or stressful situations. Say you have a near miss in your car. You sigh with relief and look up to Heaven and say thankyou. This is the moment you decided to remember your Creator. But in the mishap you may not have realized you did tap into God. Via your intuition. At extreme speed of the mishap your intuition and instinct was to think quickly. So you instantaneously tap into the Divine and get your answers. And lo and behold you avoid disaster. This all happens in the moment and hence, in the present, but to tap into the Divine means to tap into the Source which transcends and is connected to the past, present and future. This is why some people see their lives flash before their eyes in extreme situations. It is because they go to their past and future and see the wholeness and completeness of that which is God's creation…life. You exist across time and everything exists all at once. All just IS. As you would be I AM THAT I AM.

The present moment is always very real. However it is also very illusive and doesn't linger long. Before long you are onto the next moment constantly creating history which is based in the past. Forgiveness is something fitting here. As is acceptance. To completely see the present as it is and have no longing for the past and no desire for the future you are living in the present. To be aware that you are living in the present means you are in complete acceptance. Forgiveness brings you right back to the present also. Acceptance means releasing that which does not serve you anymore. Acceptance is releasement. Acceptance is liberation. Acceptance is in some cases forgiveness. To forgive is to accept and to accept is to forgive. This is a huge lesson for humankind. To be unable to forgive means you cannot accept the present. You cannot accept circumstances to be as they just are. Unforgiveness keeps you in the past and is responsible fo slowing down your experience of your present. To see how you can forgive invites in acceptance and releasement. This instantaneously brings you into the present and you feel you can see where you have been without being drawn into your past and it helps you let the future to happen TO you as opposed to trying to draw it to you faster out of controlling need. To have unforgiveness means you are completely attached and bound to the past. Tell Us, Loved Ones, how you could possibly be in the present and be ready for the future if you are tied by cords to your past? Why do you hold on so tight? We see that it is fear. You may feel angry. Yet the anger is derived from fear. Fear of not being considered. Of not getting what you feel is rightfully yours. Fear of being abandoned. Fear of the unknown.

Fear makes you look back not forward. Negative emotions prevent you from being in the present. For being in the present is the only way you can go into the future. You can't take off in once of your planes if you are not at the terminal. So too with your emotions and the present. You need to let go of that taxi which represents your past and enter the terminal. To enter the terminal means acceptance and hence you may get onto that plane which will fly into your future. Funny analogy no? It's meant to illustrate the simplicity of the concept. To stay in unforgiveness is to stay in the past and hence you cannot welcome in the future whilst being in the past. You limit and stunt yourselves. This is completely fixable. The antidote to unforgiveness is ACCEPTANCE. Acceptance is the most glorious of emotions. It is truly Godly. It is truly altruistic and empowering. To accept is to totally know that God is taking care of things and that you need to yield to His way. For His way is the only way and you, Our Loved Ones, resist total trust in God with all of your might and instead of acting in co-creation with God you try to take total control. Don't get Us wrong Loved Ones, to some degree you need to be proactive. However it is to be with co-creation with God. To listen to His guidance yet take assertive action knowing He is guiding you. To do this means to step aside from the ego and arrogance. It also means total acceptance of what is. For what is just IS. Hanging onto that which does not serve you any longer completely puts a halt on your life. It is the equivalent of a pause button. Then you sit and complain that you still feel pain. That you can never get out of this mess. Well, Our dear Loved Ones, acceptance is the only way. It is not about being foolish or gullible. It is about wisdom and knowing. You fear to know the truth and so you hide yourself from the truth which leads to feeling disconnected. To have acceptance is to have connection.

Acceptance is a way of total being. A way of releasement and at the same time challenge of that which is new. How can you fully turn to the future and embrace what it brings if you do not challenge yourself and to have total acceptance. This is the first greatest challenge for you. The thing about challenges is that they seem insurmountable, but the pride and the joy in surmounting troubles because of the effort is fully rewarding. And the reward is the ability for acceptance. Why is this the reward dear Loved Ones? Because in that moment of acceptance you realise how worth it you were, are, always will be. Forever and a day. Wouldn't that be the most amazing feeling? To know you are special in the eyes of God and yes even in your own eyes. You, dear Loved Ones, feel this feeling is illusive and unattainable. You feel this way due to feeling you are not worth it. Inadequacy. But to have acceptance lifts you and motivates you. This happens in the moment. The moment you become aware. That, Loved Ones is another good concept. Aware. Awareness. Viewing the present as it is takes awareness. How can you be aware of your present if you are still lingering in the past or gazing to the future. There is nothing wrong with this. The problem that lies in this is when you stay there. There are benefits of projecting into the future to prepare for events or goals. There are benefits of looking to the past to assess your efforts or to learn. However to stay there is a concern. Awareness helps you to resolve past issues in order to move forward. Awareness of true causes not the perceived causes. There is a difference would you believe? True forgiveness can only happen this way. The difference is that 'perceived' causes are ego driven. You may really have an issue with one person and really be angry or worse still 'hate' that person. The ego is colouring your perception of reality of the causes or stimuli. You are angered by this person and so you are going to stay angry at them and as far as you are concerned this person should come forward first. Blame and accountability are at play. But who's accountability? Usually it's six of one and half a dozen of the other. However at the time you do not always see your contribution. The day you are ready to forgive and move on is the day you completely see the reality and finally accept it and so release it and tem so you can move forward. You may finally see that that person had not acted out of malice but was just as caught up in the problem as much as you were and this may lead to you eventually getting it. Getting the fact that it was just circumstance and that heavens above you feel compassion for this person you were once angry at.

You see the beauty in them and the beauty in yourself. This is the mechanism of acceptance and perception of reality based in the heart and compassion not ego. Only the ego can get angry. The soul aside from the ego doesn't get even or angry. The soul creates catalytic energy to create change instead of building upon destructive anger. Both are motivating forces however the former is constructive, the latter is destructive. You have to choose. One way you end up repeating until you get it. The other you create releasement and healing. To release you have to forgive and to forgive you have to accept. To accept does not mean to be a doormat. To accept is to have total control without obsession. It is to know that you are in control of you and that nothing can dissuade you. Acceptance is an amazing concept of time. Before acceptance you would be suspended in time. Always looking back, not moving forward. You would be standing still and going nowhere. You would be in control of time. Yet not in a good way. You would be completely stopping your progress and ceasing your evolution. A bit like being on a footpath and heading home. You keep looking back and refuse to turn around. You keep looking back at the footpath you have already trodden on. People over take you and the sun is going down. Yet if you were to just turn your head around you would see where you are free to go next. Looking back does not mean going back. For you cannot return to the past. You cannot change the past. All that you can change is the present leading into the future. For what you do now in turn affects your future. Life is not linear it is cyclical. That includes time. As well as periods of time. Every time you look back and review your memories you are dipping back into the past. When you visualise the future and where you believe you'll be is dipping into the future hence the cyclical and interwoven aspects of time come into play. The problem lies in whether you stay in the past or future for too long. It should be a glance.

The present, as We said is the most important concept. The present is where everything happens and staying aware and present in the present reaps you great rewards. You then have the gift of seeing life as it happens before you and you have control as to what foot you put down next. Staying calm and placing all your trust in God and the Angels will fuel you forwards into your future with minimal distress. To counter stressful situations such as ill health or money woes staying in the present and dealing with things with logic will disconnect you from the emotions of worry. At least for the present. A lot of your stress has its roots in worrying about the future in the present and looking back worrying about it revisiting. As mentioned in Lisa's other book Love is an energy which powers you and gives you the validation and support you need. Turning to God leads you to Love and Love is what powers all of you. You are all Love incarnate. Love leads you to God and god is your answer. Finding your way to God is to find you way to the present and to ultimately be centred and focussed on your present and hope for your future.

The Future

The future, dear Loved Ones, is vitally important for you. The future is where you are heading and holds a great deal of promise. To behold your future and believe it will be good is encouraged. For to do this takes hope. The future is hope. The future holds hope. Hope is what takes you into the future. As you may be aware the future is not yet here and is eternally before you. Forever illusive and forever unreachable. Yet when it becomes your resent it brings with it the gifts of creation and manifestation. God wants you to go forward with hope and intention to manifest. He wants you to open your eyes like a child with total trust and hope. Expectation also. Expecting positivity. Expecting opportunities. Not with naivete but with wisdom. Wisdom which tells you that God will not give you anything you cannot handle. That whatever the future brings you have all that you need within you to deal with it.

You may have photos which have captured the past. Would it not be wonderful to have pictures which shows you your future? This would be wonderful! Then you could make decisions in the present in order to assure you a safe and prosperous future. The awareness of what the future holds is illusive and difficult to gauge. Many people seek out psychics like Lisa to find out what the future may hold. There are some variables which are easily predictable such as career or lifestyle. However there are a lot of unknowns. Be mindful that just as the present is a gift, so too is the future. God watches keenly to see which road you will walk down. For even He cannot make decision or choices for you. This is the whole point of you experiencing a human life. So that God may experience it through you. Don't forget you are a child of God. Because all exists at one moment god has awareness of what is to come and what has been. But it is an illusion. What do We mean by this Loved One? We mean that all is a mirage which is akin to a template from which you may follow. Only on the human level does it all feel tangible and physically real. It is a little like a movie script. It's all laid out on paper and yet if you are in the first scene the finish still exists, however you have not yet acted it out. Looking at your lives this way will give you a realisation that all exists at once yet occur in sequence. Hence why psychics can predict and foresee. They can tap into the layer that oversees the whole of time. Some say it's the Akashic records but that is a whole other book. We want to focus on you in the here and now and yet talking about past, present and future. The future, as We have discussed, is the cause of hope. Or hope is the cause of the future. Without hope you stay stuck in the past. Sometimes you are not even in the present.

Our dear Loved Ones We in no way are admonishing you or chastising you. All that We tell you is what you already know. We are merely highlighting this truth that you know to be true to remind you of your path. To illustrate whether you are where you are meant to be or whether you have strayed a little off your path. It is all ok. You are co-creating and evolving and be rest assured you are always going to be safe. Being a soul within a body you are experiencing a very human script. The whole point of why you are here experiencing what you are experiencing is to learn how to manage time. Note that you cannot control time but you can manage it. Keeping a brief eye on where you have come from, where you want to go but mainly where you are right now. Are you creating in the now what you always dreamt of? If your answer was no then get started! Today is a new day and We are forever waiting for your call to help and boost you in your efforts. So well done in your perseverance and tenacity. To get where you are you surely have weathered some storms. We commend you for your ability to have hope and your ability to turn negatives into positives. Nothing is wasted not even time. Never mourn your time as it never was wasted. You may not see this until you have progressed but there is no doubt that you experienced everything for a reason. The future is where you can go with the knowledge that you have gained from the past. The more you move forward with your life the more you find you have gained in knowledge. You begin to appreciate yourself. You begin to see that with age comes experience and with experience comes knowledge and with knowledge comes awareness. And with awareness you can perceive you present owning all that has gone before it. You see what has been experienced to create you as you are today. You take this with you into the future and you tuck it under your arm with purpose to use it in days to come. For in the present you are preparing for the future. Everything you have here in the now you take with you into the future. You are in ever present readiness for what is to come and to totally accept this you have to be fully present in the now and be happy to take on whatever is coming knowing full well you can cope with whatever God has in store for you. Being open and receptive is the best preparation. Love is the energy which carries you regardless of life events which happen around you. Love is all that there is. Love runs through you at all times. Even when you feel a lack of it, it is still there and yet you are somehow blocking your own access to it. For to feel the Love flowing from God source to you means you have taken away the blockages and floodgates. You are made from Love so there is never a lack of Love, there is just a blockage of Love.

There is never a cessation of Love because the energy of Love is eternal and is ever flowing throughout all that exists. Love is similar to a slip stream. It exists and is ever present but you can choose to sit on this slipstream and go where Love takes you. If you step back from the slip stream it still exists before you however you may choose to climb aboard any time. It just depends on what you want to do. If you are ready let Love take you where you aim for or if you are hesitant the watch for a while in order to decide your timing. Going with Love gets you there faster is all. You may perceive that you deny yourself Love however it is still within you. You just have a thin veil which covers it momentarily. Lift that veil and welcome Love with open arms. Love is like rain water. You can expose yourself to Love and let it saturate you. When you feel that Love is a little distant you have the equivalent of a raincoat on. Just because it is not saturating you or consuming you does not mean it is not around you.

To move into the future and have a les bumpy ride embracing this Love is the only way to move forward and welcome what is to come into your life. Love is your amour. Love is your defence. Love is you power and finally Love is you. You are Love incarnate and a willing expression of God Himself. Feel this Love as a warmth that fills you up like a warm liquid. It bubbles forth and gives you a warm feeling of self-love which you know is from you yet from some being holding you in a bear hug. Essentially it's a hug from spirit and your Angels. Feeling this will give you the feeling of total acceptance and Love. For you are loved Loved Ones. To feel this will feel cleansing. Be cleansed. For to be cleansed means to be free and ready for what is to come. For as long as you hang onto what is not serving you the longer you stay in limbo. Choose to be free and choose to move forward and accept your future. "It's not that easy" We hear you say. We know dear Loved One. We see how hard it has been for you. We have walked every step with you. Breathed every breath with you. We believe you have every right to feel cynical. However you are the only one who can live your life. A life that was given to you knowing that there is nothing you cannot handle. There will be a need at the time for you to be angry or to be disappointed and to feel it and work with it. Life will have its highs and lows and pain and joy. We cannot live your life for you. However We can guide you and support you. You will find you have gone through truly traumatic times and once you have come out of them you look back and realise what you have actually gone through and that you have survived. It is in that actual moment you realised HOW you survived and you realise We were with you all the way. The whole point of going into the future is to work on your lessons. Where would the growth be if life was totally smooth sailing? You came into your life knowing you had to have growth and the only way forward and to embrace the future is to work hard and embrace your calling.

To detach helps you to move forward. To watch and observe processes of your life and willing and wishing things to hurry up and speed along in order to relieve your impatience just does not work. In fact it actually suspends you in limbo or it delays things interminably. Lisa's favourite saying is "A watched kettle never boils". This is apt. You are holding up the process and not realising that you are ceasing your lessons from being learnt. It is not a crime. We do not chastise. We merely are just pointing it out. It's like being in a queue and constantly looking back and in the process holding up the line. There is absolutely nothing wrong with being aware of the past, however being in the present with aims of working your way towards the perceived future is the best way to be. If something is lingering and making you impatient then detachment is recommended. Detachment helps to let you use acceptance for releasement to god. The answer to counteracting the delay is to practice detachment. To observe the situation but don't be of it. To watch it with faith and know that

God Himself decides you fate. He watches every step you have taken and decides every step thereafter. He wants you to be aware of detachment and use it as a tool to help you handle the feelings of impatience and distrust. For impatience belies your distrust. Distrust taints your life experience and builds negative association. Distrust hurts you and limits you. You perceive an external stimulus to your distrust when actually distrust is really of yourself and your own choices and decisions.

To detach means to step back. To release your struggle with the topic at hand. You loosen your grip on it in order to observe it and its progress and to make a better decision based on clarity of information. Sometimes being immersed too deep in your angst can cloud your vision. How can you make decisions if your nose is too close to the screen? Step back and take it all in. This is detachment. How do you detach. In what way do you detach. You don't detach in one way or another for that denotes manipulation for personal gain. It's one attempting a skewed version of detachment based on conditions. It is conditional. Detachment is unconditional. It is basically dropping the problem totally. Stepping back and viewing it objectively. If you find this hard to do then you are not detaching. You are still trying to control outcomes. As Lisa says, be brave, let go and trust. Hand it totally over to God. Sometimes you have no choice. Sometimes you do. The times you feel hopeless and helpless is the time to surrender. This also ties in with forgiveness and releasement. But detachment is not total releasement. It is temporary releasement but with observance. It's sensing things whilst busying yourself elsewhere trusting that the road will rise up to meet you when you are supposed to get back on the path. Breathe. All of life is meant to breathe. And to pause in order to recount and survey your position. There is a strategy despite the flow of life.

Hence the future is vitally important and the preparation before going into it is vitally important. The preparation can only happen when one is aware and present. Not when one is stuck of dreaming. Dreaming is visualisation. However when you stay in that vision you remain static and it never gets actualised. Detach and go with the flow. Detachment is your way of acknowledging God's hand in this. Of yielding to His awesomeness and feeling ok to leave your issues with Him knowing full well He will never put a foot wrong. Let alone let you put a foot wrong. Not that you would. Be rest assured all things are known to Him and all things are as it is written. Even going forth into the future, as you see things they will appear new and unexpected. Where spirit is concerned all is as it should be and as planned. Even though the future has never yet been, it still is known to God. God is excited at the prospect of your discovering your future moment by moment. He never wants to ruin the surprise. However He surely does know where you are headed, whether you are aware of it or not. Whether you have chosen it or not. The future is His gift to you. Imagine the excitement in spirit at knowing what is in store. Of course you may have trepidation about negative happenings. Be mindful at the end of every storm there are rainbows. God will never let you fall.

The whole point of this book is to highlight the promise that the future holds. This is an important concept. For going into the future with optimism and hope is the only and best way to approach it. The energy of optimism and hope propels you forward. Looking back and having pessimism creates entropy. It causes you to completely stop in you tracks as far as evolution goes. Lisa akins it to the pause button on your televisions. Time stops moving the moment you look back or refuse to grow forward into your destiny. For your destiny exists and is waiting for you. Nothing is concrete and everything is fluid but one thing is certain, your future is waiting for you and you will get there. Even if you are dragged kicking and screaming. However We Angels know you'll come peacefully. See? Even We can joke. For humour and laughter is an expression of Love. Compassion allows Love to flow and allows Love to connect people together just as a switch allows the electrical current to flow. All you have to do is choose. In life all decisions are choices. You can choose to feel this way about that. Or that way about this. It's your choice. It's purely your decision whether you stay in pain or whether you release it and choose to be ok. This is not a judgement. This is a clue as to how to handle feelings and stuckness. Come on, take our hand. We'll lead you out of the unknown and into potential.

WAITING

Waiting is important. It is important to wait with a knowing. A knowing which is telling you to stay loose. To stay in readiness. To wait in readiness for what is yet to come. Waiting is different to stuckness. Waiting is a watchful hopefulness. Waiting implies non-actualised expectation and action. It's not yet actualised, yet it is potential. Meaning it is in readiness for progress and initiation. It is important to wait in readiness. God does not want you to wait forever. He just wants you to be in readiness. Then comes discernment. You are advised to have discernment as to when to wait and when to take action. All of this is acted out in the battlefield. Not that We Angels condone violence. However the image of a warrior or soldier is one of readiness and waiting. Waiting for movement, waiting for orders, waiting to go home. But all is constantly in a state of flux not stasis. Waiting shows diligence. It shows a trust in god and Us Angels. Waiting shows that you know that your Father is all knowing and benevolent. And believe it or not, it shows that you have faith in you. Faith takes time to be proven and demonstrated. But no matter what you do faith can never be disappointing. For faith brings in positivity.

Some people feel that waiting seems interminable. Boring. Worrying. Daunting. Troublesome. Irritating. However this is not 'waiting'. This is impatience. This is ego driven 'wanting'. God provides everything you need so that there is never any wanting. Only man perceives 'wanting'. And as mentioned earlier this is born of impatience. Impatience is the enemy of time. It slows time right down. In fact it makes time seem to cease. Time stands still with impatience. The progress you have made suddenly seems to disappear causing you great concern and causing more impatience and so on goes the cycle. So when you find yourself getting impatient stop, breathe and remember to come to centre and assess you situation with objectivity. Staying positive. If you get loved ones cynically telling you 'you will make the same mistake because you always do' that will keep you in stasis. Basing your present and future on their concept of the past. Just letting that thought in acknowledging it and believing it will keep you where you don't want to be. It will keep you 'waiting' for the time when you will be 'allowed' by these loved ones to actually be yourself. You don't trust yourself enough to leave their theory behind and so become their paradigm. This is NOT what your life is about or for. You are not living your life for others. You ae living it for you. Waiting for permission makes you hand over control of your life to others. Waiting is about not listening to your spiritual guidance or even to your calling. There is a time and place to take advice. However, essentially, this is your life to live and only you are at the steering wheel.

Love is not impatient. Love is patient and forgiving. Love lets you be yourself. Love is waiting for you and is with you just as your shadow is with you. It can be sensed and you know it exists but it is just to the side of you waiting and supporting. Love is the action of Godliness. Nothing exists but Love. All that you see around you is truly illusion. Love is the framework upon which all life is moulded. And Love is an expression of God. So, in essence, you are an expression of God because you are an expression of Love. Love runs through you like an electrical current and only you can switch it off and on. It is advised to keep it switched on. After all doesn't it feel good to feel Love? Love is not in a hurry. Love is always with you. Even when you are waiting. Let Us be clear dear Loved One, We are not against waiting. It is the type of 'waiting' you exercise. Sometimes waiting for the specific guidance from spirit is advisable. This is because you would be waiting in readiness. Prepared for instruction or guidance. You would have the energy of readiness for service to God. We hear laughter. Are you laughing Loved One? We are amused too. It may seem paradoxical that We are advising you not to wait then contradicting this. Remember there is active waiting and passive waiting. If you are caught in passive waiting please don't waste time in feeling guilty. There has had to be a reason why you were doing so. You probably temporarily disconnected from Spirit and God and were waiting for them to guide you. Passive waiting is disconnection. Active waiting is connection. With passive waiting you probably lost your way, lost your purpose and followed misguided signs. No matter. All is still fine in God's eyes. He smiles down upon you with knowing. Knowing that you will find you way again and that you are a willing child of God and wish only to please Him. He is pleased dear Loved One. You please Him.

Active waiting is your goal. You can do it. You HAVE done it. Active waiting is preparedness for God's word. What has this to do with time? Everything. In passive waiting it's measuring time. Every second is accounted for and watched. In active waiting it is embracing the time you have to move forward. One is watching time, the other is harnessing it. Believe it or not passive listening does have a role. It is vitally important tool that helps mankind to realise he has choices and that only he or she can make a change in his or her own life. Finding you have been passively waiting awakens to you to your behaviour which is counterproductive to your growth. You need to experience the dark to see the light. The light will guide you home. Passive waiting is sitting in stuckness and watching too hard. Active waiting is trusting and being in the moment, looking every now and then and not focussing too much on one thing. Being flexible and prepared as an athlete or a swordsman would be. Watching in order to be able to assess your next move and yet not staying long in watchfulness because eventually it will limit you. Openness and readiness. Being sure of your own ability and knowing when and how to implement it.

Human indecision and dysfunction can impede your access to the freedom of choice. In actual fact it is just seemingly so. However an obstacle nevertheless. Remember life is an illusion and that you are living out scenarios you have chosen before incarnation in order to learn. You would have given yourself time to finish these lessons and allowed time to spread out before you're waiting to be eaten up by your joy. Your joy of the gift which is your life. Embracing it and it's lessons and eager to better yourself over this allotted time. Well done for getting this far! You are truly a hero. No doubt about that. For We, dear Loved One, are your cheer squad and We follow your every move. We follow you as a new mother follows a toddler as he begins to take his first steps and brace you yet guide you unfalteringly, without too much interference. While you actively wait We wait with you and We support and encourage you. We whisper in your ear advice and guidance to help you help yourselves. For We cannot live this life for you however We understand your human time. We have given you seemingly time. Seemingly so because you have needed space to formulate your dreams and to actualise them. We know you cannot rush these things and that a job well done is a job worth doing. So if it's 'time' that you need then We will grant you that space of 'time' to do what it is that you need to do. Where We angels are there is no sense of time. Everything is there NOW. We can access what We need in an instance. And so the image of an Angel 'waiting' patiently for their charges must seem amusing considering the title of this chapter. However We are patience in motion. Patience is the friend of time whereas impatience is the enemy. Being impatient prevents you from being observant. It creates a level of risk in what you do. One wrong move and you may have to start all over again. Being present throughout all your moments of time is advisable. This might sound exhausting. However vigilance is one thing, yet active waiting is another. You are wise to have down time and not be ever ready. We will oversee you in these moments. One thing about active waiting is that it is for a reason and so is not so hard to perpetuate. When you worry you wear yourself out constantly watching with it's origins in fear. Fear makes you cling to time. It heightens your awareness of the time. When this happens time seems to slow down. Waiting has its pros and cons as you can see. Why not leave time to Us Angels?

WISHING

Ah now We come to 'wishing'. Wishing is the epitome of positive thinking and optimism. It is how We want you to live you lives. Wishing means knowing there is a time to come. This time to come is the future. Knowing this time to come means anything could happen yet you are open to something good happening. This is crucial for living in the moment. Living in the moment whilst wishing leads to time and its measurement disappearing. You have totally released it to Us. Wishing means you only see good for you in the future. Wishing is wanting only good for you in the future. Wishing is the backbone of manifestation. And, dear Loved One, manifestation does exist. You practice is constant and constantly it is fulfilled. How? We hear you ask. Well dear Loved One....wishing for a bus to turn up early and it does. Wishing for your son to come home safe, and he does. Manifestation happens in every moment of your human time. In your everyday lives. It is the script for which you are to learn your faith in God by. Manifestation, and the practice of it, makes the world go around. It's how you live minute by minute, hour by hour and day by day. Manifestation is the act of working with God in improving your life and it works in tandem with hope, faith and trust. It never ceases and goes on forever. Hence it is timeless and rises above time as you know it. It is essential that manifestation straddles time. Manifestation is in perpetual vacillation between the present and the future. Even drawing upon the past if need be to assess what needs to be brought into your life which is no longer a lesson but a gift. The Angels of manifestation work hard to constantly create reality for you. They are constantly waiting and watching and placing experiences or encounters before you with eager devotion. You say the word and they will bring it to you. However what is brought to you may be in your higher interest. So be warned, if you have not learnt your lessons what is manifested may be along the lines of what you have asked for, but may be in another form in order for the lesson to be picked up and resumed. You're not getting away that easy Loved One! The angels of Manifestation have eagle eyes. They cannot be fooled. They hear your wishes. They look at your level of evolution. They see if it is a genuine need aligned with your purest of intent. Then they bring into play the result. Spirit are not cruel and do not want to cause angst for you. Spirit can only work within the parameters you set for them yourselves. They want to give you everything you ask for. However there are no short cuts. If you try to manifest without putting in effort the response from Spirit is one that may not be complete in your estimation. However this is not Spirit's fault. In fact Spirit may have tried to warn you not yet. They may have tried to let you know you need to go a little way further before manifestation can be complete.

You may feel it is them who are being obstructive. Not so, Loved One, for it is you who is obstructive. Awareness of this releases you and moves things along more quickly. Wishing for things to happen is advisable and admirable. For it shows you are being optimistic and willing to serve God. This is good. This is what is meant for you. Wishing is a gift to yourself. Wishing means you only want the best for yourself and that you expect good things. Wishing actually brings things towards you. This is why wishing is integral to manifestation. Not only that, manifestation is integral to wishing. To intend to manifest you need to wish. In order to have a wish you have to understand manifestation. Although this is not a hard and fast rule. Wishing with innocence and not manipulating things for you own outcomes is also recommended. Meaning, that to innocently wish for something without intent for personal gain and no motive or awareness of manifestation because you just trust spirit can still bring results. This is because your innocence ensures purity of intent and selflessness. Dear Loved Ones We by no means are judging or berating you. We merely are illustrating scenarios from which you can see where you may have gotten thoughts from. Information is invaluable and if you can find a reliable paradigm you may find this eases your woes. We Angels see mankind and womankind as perfection. We know what you are capable of, good and bad and in between. Essentially We see you as good. Good people who sometimes wander off God's chosen path for you. Even so We see a lot of good. You are after all made after your Creator and your DNA is of God Source. So you are spiritual, holy souls having a very Earthly and human experience. We Angels do not agree with chastising you for your sins or your wrong doings. We, in representation of God, love you regardless and totally. We adore you and our intention of alerting you to your so called 'sins' is to help you straighten up and fly right. No pun intended. Sins are not a sign of evil. It is a sign that you have lost your connection to the God Source and have inadvertently erred along the way. The reason why We alert you to it is because We can see you are heading for hurt. Sins are titles of the deeds which you do that do not serve your higher purpose. Sins are merely diversions from your true path. Keep aiming high, dear Loved One, for one day you will soar. Do not forget to keep wishing.

Wording

Wording for wishing is important. In order to harness your time wishing ties into the tie line and accesses the energy of manifestation. Wording is vital in manifestation and wishing. For it is in the action of 'asking' you appeal to spirit to help you along your way. For without asking how would you progress? Please ask Us. We are sitting on the edge of Our seats awaiting your call. Ask and you shall receive. For how can things move forward out of stuckness without at least initiating things by asking?

When you think of what to ask you become aware or wording. As Lisa has found, We make her write and rewrite certain passages because We want to be sure of creating the right concept. She has been most frustrated with Our insisting that she rewrite a passage because We feel it won't convey the right feeling. It's important that We do this because words convey energy and can influence your thoughts and eventually your outcomes. Sometimes negatively, but mostly positively. So hence We strive for positive influence. Wording in your prayers usually are spontaneous and appropriate in the moment. You can never word it wrong. Just as Lisa is not wording things wrong. There is a difference in writing a book and saying a prayer…..but not by much. When you pray to God and Us Angels We hear what you are saying and take it on board. If you can't find the right words We understand anyway because We feel where the imploring comes from. We know what you are truly wanting. We know how urgent and necessary your queries are. No doubt about it you are important to Us and We love you so We want only the best for you. However in manifestation of truly serious nature wording is the most important aspect to be aware of.

What has this to do with time? We hear you ask. Everything. For not asking and not wording mindfully will hold things up for you. It won't affect Us as We sit and wait in attendance. However We sit in waiting on every word you say to give you your heart's desire. This is where you can use words to your advantage. If you think carefully before you ask. This is why ritual is a good idea. The planning and carefulness of preparations is akin to what We are talking about. The meditative state before a ritual leads to a mindfulness which shows intent. This, Our Loved One, is a powerful action.

Why would Angels be talking about ritual? Ritual is in all religions and belief systems. None of them are sacrilegious. Unless they belong to the dark. This phases Us not. For We are the biggest club there is. For We are talking about ritual of any kind including, you may be surprised to hear, alternative. If it is for the higher good and only for good then We do not discriminate. Ritual leads to a peaceful state of wishfulness and manifestation. Ritual and prayer taps into the eternal. Meaning that it reaches across time and is timeless. However it brings to you what you need in the present. Specificity is important. In asking for help and for positive outcomes wording is important in asking. For, as the saying goes, you get what you ask for. Literally. This is hoped to be fun. Like asking Father Christmas what you want for Christmas. You know exactly what you want. To ask for something that you can take into the future with you. It may be a job. Or a house. Or love. Not a hint of greed but more like need. Your role is to trust in God and know that when the time is right manifestation will take place. If what you want does not appear straight away then it must not be the right timing. There's that illusive word, time, again.

For choosing the right wording will get you on the right path. Manifestation does not necessarily bring it straight to you. Instead it puts you on the right path towards it. The propulsion is your own devotion and applying of your own energy and motivation. You have the motive god gives you the means. Every little feeling of doubt is felt by spirit. Saying correct wording with appropriate motivation and little doubt gets the access to manifestation happening quicker. Here comes into play the concept of time and how it relates to ritual and prayer. Things seem to go quicker and things fall into place when you come from a sincere need and lack of ego. When you resist your own growth and evolution you find that time seems to slow right down and you get frustrated with the process and even with spirit. You may feel fatigued and bewildered and not sure how much longer you can go on. As soon as you acknowledge and not resist your lessons you can move forward into the future and time will seem to move again. Remember that time is a human concept. And fast and slow moving time is an illusion. However We Angels can work within these constraints. All is valuable. Each moment of time is valuable and important. No mistaking that.

Taking the time to word your prayers carefully causes a flow to happen. Lisa akins it to a transaction. You ask and literally We give. It is not that concerning. We, of course, are aware of the variables. We then give you hints to make sure you are certain this is what you want. Gradually you learn to pick up on these hints and utilise them to your advantage. Be mindful your life is a team effort. You're never alone. Every word We hear. In your prayers say your heart's desire. Open with absolute faith and trust in spirit and never be afraid spirit won't hear you. See how you would be expected by spirit to do your part in helping them to help you. Be completely in service to spirit as they are to you. Talk to them and they will speak to you. Give and they will give back. You are a warrior and so is spirit. Forging ever forward determined in your stance to conquer all obstacles before you. All on the power of words.

Fulfilment

There is not doubt about it that fulfilment is the goal here. Believe Us, Loved One, it is mutual. You're receiving your goals through prayer and wising and manifestation is fulfilment for you as it is for Us Angels and spirit. For you it is completion of a cycle of need, prayer and action. For Us and spirit it is fulfilment of our roles as your protectors and providers. Having said that only God provides. We are just agents for God and We devotedly assist in this process of providing for you. Fulfilment is the goal and is always attainable. Anything is possible. There is a recipe for you to follow and sometimes you stray. That is ok. All part of the journey. It is not a bad thing to wander off the path here and there. In fact God designed it that way. Life would be very boring if it was all in one direction. Meandering off track provides the growth your soul so craves in order to find your way home again. Going with the flow and learning how not to stray again is all part of the picture and it can be fun.

We Angels know how hard life can be for you on the Earthly plain. We know there are many challenges and sometimes traumas. Life is like a school yard. A necessity for growth warts and all. Many knocks and bumps. But also many joys. Only time will tell. Living through this school of life is living through time. Time is measured on Earth and it is important that it is. Time creates a backdrop to where you have come from and where you intend to go. Without this measuring device you cannot learn anything. Time is symbolic for the path with which you achieved your fulfilment. It gives you a guideline with where to start and where you will end up. Fulfilment is sweet sweet victory. We Angels rejoice in your celebration of achieving it. However We rejoice in all that you do. Fulfilment brings with it an awareness of what you have learnt and what you have achieved. Some things came about as planned and yet others came about out of left field and not planned at all. Yet in hindsight you will see that all painted the picture of what your life is now. None was wasted nor was it wrong. Even if unplanned it was still a part of the process. Fulfilment is the final destination of a particular phase of your life. Fulfilment is actualisation. Actualisation is when you have accomplished all you are working towards. Actualisation is full recognition of your Godliness. That God is perfect and in actualising your dreams and goals for fulfilment is when you are fully recognising that God is working through you and that is perfection. Keeping it humble and knowing that God is the ultimate. You as humans are perfect in creation, yet not yet perfect in actualisation. This is your assignment on Earth.

Love is behind fulfilment. Being in touch with Love carries you forth towards fulfilment. Love's goal is to manifest fulfilment. Love will never carry you astray. Love sees everything and nothing ever eludes Love's gaze. For Love works on behalf of God and as you know, God sees everything and misses nothing. This is to reassure you that you are never alone not to intimidate you. It tells you that there is bound to be a positive outcome and no matter what your life is happening on God's watch. He Himself makes certain that outcomes create fulfilment of lessons and life's roles. All of this happens over time and during your life 'time'. Time is important in fulfilment because it symbolises the time needed to act out these life lessons for the final outcomes. None of your lessons could be completed without awareness of time. Not only do you need the time to apply the lessons, but time fives you space to create and produce results. Time – past, present and future provide a structure, a framework to build upon and a depth of room to rebuild your lives and interweave your lessons within that. Looking back at your past gives you inspiration and insight. Time is fulfilling God's expectations for you. Every moment is pregnant with awe inspiring Godly creation and learning. Not one thing is a waste. Ever. Fulfilment provides relief, reward and satisfaction. Keep striving for fulfilment as it always keeps you focussing forward not back. You will have fulfilment because We Angels will see to it.

Needing

Need is a desire based in necessity. Needs are highly important. You as humankind naturally have immediate needs. All living animals have needs. Needs are what God provides for. He created you to have needs as needs are the currency for growth. Needs facilitate growth. For growth to happen there needs to be a stimulus. A need. Is that clear Loved One? Ha ha. We know We repeat ourselves. We will endeavour to explain until We say it so you can absorb it. The most important need a living being has is for Love. Love is after all what makes the world go around no? Believe it or not you were designed to have needs. For it forces you to live in the moment with intent on moving into your future and claiming your birthright……Heaven.

That is right Loved One, We said Heaven! Heaven is not ever denied you. You have always been entitled to it and nothing can stop you from achieving it. It is, however, your goal and where you are aiming for. It is not going to fall into your lap Our dearest One. It is, however, your goal and where you are aiming for. It is not going to fall into your lap Our Dearest One. It has to be worked towards. It is the ultimate in outcomes. It is home. It is where needs no longer exist because everything is One in Heaven. There is no need as it is a place of being which is fully actualised. It is where you are from and where you will go back to. So never fear Loved One you are never far from home. You have merely gone out into the street to play. God will call you to home again when you are ready and completeness has happened.

Needs are essential in gaining your skills. They drive you forward in order to survive and in doing so create the amazing, accomplished person you are. You will look back to your past and see that if it weren't for your need for shelter and sustenance you wouldn't have achieved your skills in acquiring both. Such as finding a home, and a job. All survival skills you now have and now you can safely say you can fulfil those needs. See aren't you an amazing child of God? We want you, dear Loved One, to use your needs. Yes you heard Us correctly. Use. Use your awareness of a need to harness the earnest desire. For harnessing earnestness is the only way. Then doing two things at once. Asking for what you need, then willing it to be so with – earnestness. This word symbolises your truest needs. Your most honest needs. For this is the only currency you need for manifestation. You cannot gain from greed based perceived 'needs'. It just won't happen. Being humble and earnest in your needs will draw to you the most benevolent of helping energies. You, in that moment, will be in touch with your creator. There is not a need that goes unanswered. You may be saying "but I asked for such and such! How come it never happened?". Simple dear Loved One, it was not an earnest need. This does not mean you are never going to have that need met. This just means there are higher needs that need meeting for you of which you may not be focussed on. All in the course. Loved One don't fret and don't doubt. Stay focussed. All will come in time. Do not get ahead of yourself or of Us. It can cause you unnecessary grief.

You would not be human if you had no needs. For the very fact you are human says that you chose this life to learn life's struggles deriving from need. No need is too small or too big. The desire for the need is the only variant. You may desire strongly or weakly. Yet the need stays the same. It is your perception of how urgent the need is. Only God Himself may deem it necessary for immediate action. However be sure of one thing, Loved One, that is WILL be met. All of your life is in place and there are many plans in place for its destiny. You can bet that spirit have already got plans in place for whatever circumstance arises. There is not one need which does not have an answer for it. Lisa is amused as We have shown her a list symbolising how all needs are itemised. We like this as Lisa has a sweet sense of humour. She reads for others with Humour and strength for which that person may need. This is why We bring the issue up. Lisa has communication skills designed for helping others and she uses humour and strength to put her point across. This hits its mark much more succinctly. It provides an answer for the client's need. She is right now wondering why We are bringing her into this. It is because We have chosen her. She is dear to Us and speaks for Us in only her own unique way. Therefore, it brings results. Her clients, Our Loved Ones, needs are met through her services. We are using her as an example. She followed a calling to help others as she keenly felt their needs for reassurance and Love. She is a channel for Love. She is doing what she was always meant to do. For she had needs too. She is a channel for Love. She is doing what she was always meant to do. For she had needs too. Now she is giving to those who need. Forgive Us Lisa for exposing you like this. We love you.

HOPE

Here We get to Hope. Hope is the next most powerful emotion next to Love and yet is so fleeting. Or seemingly so. Both Love and Hope can seem elusive and out of reach. However once attained are both powerfully transformative. It's akin to finding the slip stream which takes you off smoothly on your path and makes everything seem easy. It feels tenuous. However, once found and felt it is incredibly powerful and empowering. Hope is fuel for propulsion. It is the desire to exclude and evict feelings of negativity and pessimism. Hope is the utilisation of 'time' for your own benefit. Have you ever thought of it this way Loved One? That while you worry you are eating up moments of time? It only takes a moment to wish and pray with Hope. However worry eats up your precious time and creating a vicious cycle of worry –delay – pain – deterring – worry. Let go of worry Loved One. For it is getting you nowhere as you can see! Can you not see the wasted of time that worry is? We in no way want to diminish genuine worry, however even with genuine need and worry there still should come a point where you leave it in order to move forward in time to get past it. This is where Hope takes place. Hope transcends time. Hope can move you through time. It has the effect of a bridge across time. Should you take the path of Hope it will lift you up over the stream of worry.

To feel Hope, We are sure you have felt this before, is to feel empowered and uplifted. In that moment you are not thinking of the past. You are only focussed on going into the future yet feeling very much in the present. It is all about creation and creation can only happen in the moment, in the present. Creation is like a train which has destination 'future' in its sights. To be able to create you have to have the enthusiasm which can only come from Hope. Creation is an energy which moves you forward on and on. For to start a creative process you have to see it through to the end. This means opening p to the freedom of timelessness. Releasing time constraints and not perceiving time. Surely you have memories of being very engrossed in something and the time just flew? This is what We mean Loved Ones. Time disappears, at least seemingly so. You have no more need for time or the measurement of it. You are just 'doing'.

Isn't Hope wonderful thing? Hope is also very Angelic. We Angels are living examples of Hope. We inject it into you at those times when you can't seem to access it. It's always there of course, however you may wander away from it and so end up not sensing it nearby. Searching for Hope sometimes can be a lifelong search for some. They don't feel deserving and attempt to find Hope yet give up too early and reinforcing their own perceptions that Hope is illusive and not for them. Hope is only for those who deserve they may think. Not so. Hope is what the Universe runs on. Remember, it is closely related to Love. Love is actualisation of Hope. You could say Hope is the road leading to Love. You all will have, and one day will again, walk this path and actualise your dreams. Actualisation is not an elusive thing that happens to only a select few. Actualisation is something that everyone has experienced. In this life and in other lives, past and yet to come. We will talk about actualisation soon.

So dear Loved One, you can see that Hope is very important in this process. The lack of Hope keeps you in limbo and you feel you see no way out. The superstars you see on your televisions had Hope. How do you think they got there? It was untainted Hope. Pure Hope which had a silent 'knowing' about it that told them they would make it one day. Having said that you all do have special roles in this life and your time this time around may have been specific and not necessarily fame intended. There are many happy silent workers committed to helping behind the scenes. Whose only glory is seeing their hard efforts coming to fruition and helping others find their way. Hope is knowing that you are doing what you are supposed to be doing right now at this moment in time and that whatever you will be doing in the future you will know in time, but you hope it is all good. It will be. Hope makes it so. Never give up Hope. For it will never give up on you.

Giving

Now here is an act of Love if ever there was one. Giving. God gives to you everyday. Without expectation or demands. He knows its all part of the process and gives willingly with Love as He knows you are His children and He would do anything for you all. It is altruistic and genuine. He does not demand reciprocation. He just wants His children to live and love with all of their might. His outlook is Giving without demand. Giving totally and happily. He sets an example and gladly so. He gets great joy out of watching your lives and avidly takes in all that you do with Love.

To Give is one role of being human. To get to a space where you no longer need more, more, more but where you feel joy in just giving because you have all that you need in your life…..your relationship with God and the Angels. Feeling the freedom to be able to Give is when you have let go entirely of time. Time still exists and yet you are just 'in' it. You're not a chasing it or regretting it. You are happily in the moment, the present, listening to the voice of God keenly and all with a smile on your face as you happily just give. No strings attached. Just giving. This is peace. It brings peace. Peacefulness makes you feel suspended in time and that you are not a prisoner of time constraints. You are free and independent. You feel a sense of timelessness because you are not watching it constantly. You are too busy living life. Not measuring or comparing. Hence Giving is not just to others. It is also about Giving to yourself. How can you give to others if you can't Give to yourself? Giving is the energy of life. It flows from you when you feel free to do so. Giving provides motivational energy and facilitates others to move forward in time. Your Gift may actually make someone's future brighter. You cannot do anything about the pat but you can help improve the future.

Your goal is to get to where you feel ok to feel Hope in order to be able to Give. Giving shows you have completely let go of your expectations and the time concept. For time, as We have already discussed, is just an illusion. A concept of measuring moments in order to gauge what was once and what will be. To give is not to just give to others, although this is admirable. It is also the act of yielding to God. Giving to God everything with absolute trust. Giving over the power to God. Being human you sometimes forget or don't realise that God is all that there is. True there are some things which you are needed to take charge with on your own. However life is forever a dance of embracing responsibility and then yielding. You are the ones who have to find the rhythm in hand with God. Sometimes it is you sometimes it is Him. You are the apprentice where some initiative is encouraged and when you stop to scratch your head in a quandary then that is when God steps in to prompt. Giving means being willing to give to God in these moments and letting go of pride or fear. Completely yielding to the process.

To do the same for another is a gift that has a ripple effect. Giving to someone else, whether money, possessions or just time, this helps them in their own process of helping others. So on and so forth. Therefore Giving is timeless. For it goes on into the future rippling out and touching all who go thereafter. Giving is also connected to Love and Hope. To give to someone is to have hope that will bring about assistance for them. The act of this is done in Love and as you know by now all of Love is from God. When you act out of Love you act from your Creator. So to give is to be of a Godly way and manner. God would be proud. He is anyway but this is one thing God takes pride in. That His children have enough Love in their hearts to make it possible to Give something away.

Give freely. Give with your heart. Keep giving. For if you Give knowing what goes around comes around then you are in the process of manifestation. You are being bold in expecting only the best. Doubt is a person's worst enemy. It can disable you quicker than a car immobiliser. Completely stop you in your tracks. For you see, Loved One, this is how you get in your own way. Quite simple really. Never fear for God gives you many options to straighten up again. Lisa has a saying that she uses often. A duck on water looks simple and moving smoothly, yet under the water busy as ever, this is what spirit is like. Illusion on the surface yet a lot of activity and effort behind the scenes. This illusion is necessary for it helps to prevent you becoming overwhelmed at all that goes on. It helps you to just focus on the task at hand. Leave your worries with Us dear Loved Ones. We will carry you when you cannot carry yourself. You are very hard on yourself sometimes. We don't want you to linger on this negative thought. Move beyond and above it. You are worth more than self-blame and hatred. You are beautiful and when We see you We see your light. Literally. We see the white light which emanates from you. Those who are with the dark are also glowing with white light yet have the cloak of darkness over it which they themselves have draped over their shoulders. This can be removed.

Time being around you past, present and future, means that you are forever living within it. Any act of giving within time gives you momentum through time. As mentioned before Giving goes on into the future, but have you thought that giving is also from the past. For all that has gone before you has built the structure and framework from which you work form within your own life. For you would not have what you have now if giving had not happened somewhere prior to your existence. We, dear Loved One, do not mean that you have not been responsible for your accomplishments. We know how hard you have worked at your achievements and they are there as badges of honour. What We are saying is that people before you were incarnated built cities, jobs, belief systems and ways of existence which help you even today and keeps giving to you. Such things as medicine, law, education, familial legacies. All were given by your predecessors with aims that their descendants would benefit by their creations. All God inspired. However their accomplishments nonetheless. See how man can work with God to Give?

Actualisation

We have mentioned Actualisation many times before but let Us now focus more closely on it. Actualisation is the ultimate for a person. It means becoming who you desire or are meant to be by attaining all your goals in evolution. You start off at one point in time, you birth, and end up where you are meant to be at the end of your life as actualised. So Actualisation also spans across time. Actualisation is when you know you have achieved what you incarnated to achieve. This manifests on the physical but most importantly on the emotional and mental. For you experience the world on all these levels. However the most important level is spiritual. To Actualise your life's purpose means that spiritually you have been listening to your guidance and to your connection to God. For ultimately this is what God wants for you is to Actualise yourself. It is, let Us say, your assignment on this plane of existence. All is controlled from above as your lives are in god's hands yet it is only so in co-creation with you. You have sports people on the Earthly plane who need trainers or coaches. Neither one is above the other, however one oversees the other because they have their back. One cannot exist without the other.

You are born with an innate need to find your destiny. Your destiny is truly your Actualisation. If this involves relationships, children and careers along the way then so be it. Actualisation is probably the closest topic We will talk about in this book which is close to measurement of time itself. For it is something that while you are busy aiming to accomplish it you just move through time just existing in the present dealing with what comes with the present yet it's taking you on into the future with intent for a future outcome. Preferably rewarding. Ah, but child, all is rewarding. However you need to feel that there is a reward there for you and We are more than happy to oblige by giving you inspiration. Measuring where you've come from and where you are going to by aiming for actualisation keeps you busy focussing on getting there. We are not talking about lingering on the past as such, more that you may observe and learn from past errors or gains and using that to propel you forward to claim your future with gusto.

The Wisdom of Time is about knowing that all is one and nothing is separate. To actualise your dreams and goals is to give the biggest gift to yourself. You have allowed yourself to transcend time and to live in the now drawing on the past in order to create in the future. Actualisation is the result of manifestation. Creating is what you are meant to do. Creation goes beyond God's reach, but with a purpose. He designed it that way. He, the ultimate in Creators, wishes for you to create and with your own free will.

Joy

Sometimes you long for something strongly and wish it to be so now and so become a pawn between past and future and bounce around like a ping pong ball within your emotions. All the while resisting the present. Frightened if you look at it you will see a lack. There is never a lack all that you desire is coming. They all just have different ETAs. Joy is the feeling you feel when you accept the here and now. Joy is a releasement and liberation. It releases you from dread and worry and misperception. Being in the feeling of Joy you feel the Love of God within you and working through you. This is purely because all the heavy feelings you may have had blocked that and now by accepting the present as it is it frees you up and you can see clearly. It has the metaphorical equivalent of being lifted up by a crane to see the path ahead as from your original standpoint you may have only seen five feet in front of you.

Joy is what you feel when you completely open to the channelling of God's Love within and through you. Don't forget Loved One that you are a child of God and so have Him within you. Joy is inbuilt into your children and is a feeling which bubbles through them naturally because they have not yet learnt to block or control it. We of course recognise that there is a time and a place for it when you are adults but please We beg of you to have a joy button within you so you may press it when the time is appropriate. Lisa is laughing with joy as she has just thought f something to illustrate Our discussion and she will tell you it's a vision of a computer which you buy with already downloaded software. This what you are like as newborns. Good analogy no? you are already pre-programmed with God's Love and the Joy resulting from that knowledge of you having Joy within you. With Love you may have already experienced it through your relationships. Your family, friends, partners or children. Even with animals. All is relevant and none it wasted. All are lessons along the way to love yourself as you love those around you. Animals give you that window glimpse into the truth of what Love is. They are pure Love and give it to you with hopes that all you ever will do with them and others and with yourself, is Love in return. Be mindful there are different ways to Love someone. It can be about giving your all to someone if you feel safe to. However Love is also shown in the form of standing strong and having strong boundaries where you are open to change and someone venting yet with a strong centredness where you show compassion and that you are present but not being gullible. You see Love is soft and reassuring but it also can be tough. You can love someone even when they behave badly but you stay strong and show it by having strong boundaries yet being present with them. It is what you may call tough love. Love manifests in many ways and does not mean naïve blind love which leaves you vulnerable. At least not immediately. There is such a thing as self-love which you should have first and this acts as a filter for other's love and where it stems from. Genuineness or greet. Joy is the expression of Love once it has been frisked and let through the barrier. Again Lisa's laughing at the image. Is not humour an expression of Joy? We, dear Loved One, want you to love freely but to do so with wisdom and then Joy.

Being Joyful and optimistic is forward thinking and progressive in behaviour. There's not a single person who doesn't dream of a positive future. The only problem is when you look back in fear worrying that what has gone before will happen again. Staying positive and forward thinking brings a good future towards you. Releasing what you have known in trust that only good fortune will come is more likely to attract to you your true path on which you feel in control and satisfied. Sitting in Joy gives you the feeling of liberation which frees spirit up to create for you the outcome you desire. Yes it may seem all that happens is dependent on you well, dear Loved One, it is. This does not mean you have failed at times. Far from the truth. You have succeeded and you will see in hindsight that all was as it was mean to be and all added to the mix out of which evolves the complete you that you will be or are about to become.

Don't ever let go of Joy. For it is always with you and is ever present. All you have to do is to connect with it and access it. Lisa is suggesting it is like an app. Always there ready to use and yet dormant in those who don't yet realise they have it close at hand. It never ceases. It just gets overlooked at times. Joy is abundant and is born of wisdom. It fuels and motivates you to get out of stuck points and We encourage you to access it and use it. Joy lifts you up and is pure power. You are amazed at this statement? Have We not mentioned that there is only strength in listening to God? That to do so means you are tapping into the ultimate Power? What comes from God? Love and hence Joy. Joy is not naivete or gullibility. Joy is wisdom in action. Those who are joyful see all that there is and are positive regardless because they know that is the only way to break through. They see that they can rise about trouble and go beyond it. Hanging onto Joy, even in the most desperate of times, ensures that you are not conquered or abandoned. If you feel abandoned it is purely because you have tuned God and Spirit out. He is still there and will never leave. He is simply on the other side of the veil. Tapping into Joy is akin to hopping onto His wavelength. A bit like when you tuned into your favourite radio station. Once you find the right wavelength you will know what We mean about Joy. Joy is power. Joy is creative power. Joy is your power.

Inspiration

Inspiration is gleaned from Joy. Once you are in that place of Joy you will find it leads to Inspiration. We want to talk about Inspiration as way of harnessing Joy and using it to move you forward. Imagine you feel Joy, what is it that it leads to in regards to your thoughts? It leads to ideas and dreams no? Joy is the fuel and Inspiration is the means to gain your life's goals and dreams. You feel Inspired. To be inspired means you have finally let go of the past and looked to the future and left behind negative self-talk. It's not wrong to be in a negative space it merely doesn't serve you to be there. We, after all dear Loved One, support you at all times. We never leave We are but on the other side of the veil. Some of you believe We Inspire you. This is true sometimes. However mainly it is you who inspires you. You find what it is that is your hearts desires and aim for it. We Inspire you in showing you that all is possible in the eyes of God. Remember that. All is possible in the eyes of God. Aspiring to raise yourself to your Father gives you Inspiration and Joy. Joy is the wave you ride in order to get to your Father. Inspiration is the idea to do so. You all need ideas to work from. To manifest from. To have a goal and focus for where your life is heading. Ideas are sometimes under rated in mankind. They can be seen as frivolous and idealistic. All of your visionaries started with ideas. Your scientists, architects, artists, politicians, teachers, writers, students and musicians. Inspiration forms in your heart and manifests in your mind and together they fuel the desire to bring it to fruition. You then tap into Spirit to access divine assistance. This divine assistance gives you that extra force to bring it on home. We in spirit see this idea germinate in your ore and watch it grow and evolve. We look on with joyful anticipation as it grows and becomes more actualised and hope that you call on Us to give you that extra help to really make the idea stand out.

Inspiration raises you above and once you get a scent of inspiration it has the power to make worries dissolve away. You suddenly have clarity and feel free from the constraints of perceived time. It drives you onward and upward and you suddenly can see your future and where you are capable of getting to. All becomes clearer and attainable. Inspiration also seems to come along with intuition. You may perceive an idea in your mind with a gut feeling that it seems very real and possible. You all of a sudden have a vision of how you can attain this idea and goal. It seems to open up before you. Inspiration may be spontaneous and in the moment. Other Inspiration may be long term as in childhood dreams that you wait for the right time to implement.

Inspiration is a 'knowing' that comes to you with a feeling of upliftment and Joy which opens up your mind and imagination to potentialities and hopes and dreams. Suddenly, as you embrace it, they Inspiration opens doors to your full imagination and gives you vision to see exactly what you are capable of. Inspiration is Godlike. What We mean is that tapping into Inspiration is really tapping into your God Source. You ae tapping into the Source of all that IS. It is truly Heaven sent. We, dear Loved One, wish for you to have been Inspired by this book. We wish to Inspire and uplift. We see that Inspiration is infectious. For a truly Inspired person is Inspirational to be around. They lead the way for others who seek it. They show how it has affected them and touched their lives. It shows that if one person has it then any other person can have it. Inspiration naturally associates itself with Hope and Joy. It leads to manifestation and actualisation. To be inspired is to be future focused by living in the now. Inspiration means seeing what can be brought forth for your future and yet is in creation now. It is the doorway to claiming your future and the events that come with it that you have created and wished for. It leads you forth to take each step bravely and to grasp that dream that has always seemed so far off into the distance.

Inspiration is also the feeling of knowing your Creator is with you. To have Him enter your body is to feel Inspired and enlightened. You feel like you have His power within you and this can be harnessed in order to climb above the dross. Inspiration is God. God is all that there is and to realise that you have god with you and hence Inspiration means you claim your birthright to being enlightened and aware. To be with god is to have awareness. To have awareness means you see all that goes on around you and that with this you are able to surmount anything. This means you are transcending time and seeing all that is around you as opposed to fixating on past or future alone. Inspiration is transcending. It raises you up and allows you a bird's eye view of your time on Earth. Reading any spiritual books and scripts or even the Bible are uplifting and Inspirational. Remember that what you read can lift or lower your vibration. If you focus on uplifting and positive spiritual writings this will bring and keep you to the spot where inspiration exists and frees you up to create. Your thoughts are lighter and more positive and you start to believe you can do anything. Doubt leaves your vocabulary and you become optimistic and productive. Follow God follow Us Angels. We will lead the way and god will welcome you home.

KNOWING

Ah dear Loved One, We feel by now from reading this book you are feeling a 'Knowing' coming on. A knowing that is enveloping you and lifting you up. That is the intention. Lisa likens this type of book to form of meditation. As you read it you go into a place that is sacred and peaceful. You transcend the worries and concerns of the day and almost sit in prayer as you read a spiritual book. We intended this book as a prayer and contemplation. As you read you find a spot within that suddenly finds peace and a connection to your God. This is because you are finding a Knowing. A Knowing that god is within you and yet even with you at that very moment watching you read and attending keenly to you as each word penetrates and hits home. He sits beside you as benevolently as a parent does with a child at bedtime reading a children's book. He bangs on every word that you read and hopes and sees every word means something to you. Knowing implies that you have actualised what you've learnt from the past and ready and willing to look to the future to apply this Knowing. Knowing means you are ready to move forward not hang onto the past. Gaining knowledge is why man has been created. So that God may experience this 'Knowing' through you and to express Himself manifest. He gets amazing joy from experiencing your joy and is proud of your accomplishments. There is not a thing you can do that would drive Him from you and He is with you always. Knowing this is what frees you.

To know that you have nothing to fear a no one can take away this connection to God is to have complete mastery of your fears and claim to your destiny as God's child. To live in God's kingdom knowing that all was for a reason and knowing that all was as it was meant to be. Knowing is a crucial milestone. It shows education is complete in that particular category. Of course learning never stops, yet in your lifetime you come to learn in order to know what is specific to that lifetimes lessons. Knowing is complete acceptance of God's way and complete immersion in His word. Knowing brings what was once into the past into the present to prepare you and arm you for the future you are destined to inherit. Knowing is something that can only be attained over time. Some children are born Knowing. This is due to their having lived many a lifetime and gaining a Knowing from living lifetime after lifetime. You too have lived before and your Knowing reflects the shadows of those past lifetimes. Knowing is what you bring with you from your past and carry as light to illuminate the way into the coming future. You measure your knowledge with you projection into the future and gauge possible outcomes in order to navigate your life. Yet those people who have a true Knowing may not always have the need to project or predict. They usually are content in the moment and happy to let the road rise up to meet them.

Knowing is not selective and is very mutual. It arises in all of you. It is one of your birthrights. It is why you ae here. Knowing is energy from God Source and powers you all through your lives accumulating as you go. Knowing, dear Loved One, is already installed in you. We will wait while Lisa composes herself. This obviously amused her. You are pre-programmed with Knowing and this Knowing helps you to survive. Some may call it instinct. Knowing is being tuned in and getting the message instantaneously and applying counter moves. There is a Knowing which is inbuilt and automatically available. This is your pure connection to spirit and most importantly to God. Knowing brings peace to you because you see that all life continues and, despite life's travails, you know that another day will come, another lesson will be dealt with and you know you will survive. Most importantly your Knowing means you Know God and yourself.

Manifestation

Manifestation is the ultimate outcome and goal in one's life. Manifestation speeds up as you learn your lessons and mature. Once you have let go of trivialities and concerns which take up a lot of your time and energy, the flow of manifestation frees up improves. Never worry that you will never have this for it is guaranteed that you will experience it in your lifetime. It is not a matter of 'if' it's a matter of 'when'. Manifestation We have mentioned frequently in this book and it is what We desire the most for you. Manifestation is what you grow towards and as you get more experienced the easier it is to create it. Manifestation is possible once one has gotten rid of doubt, fear, self-loathing and anger. Manifestation is always there around you ready to tap into however you have to learn to reach up for it. Belief is key to obtaining it for if you don't believe it's possible to actualise your dreams then you won't know to reach for it.

Manifestation is an ongoing process and works in all areas of life. From manifesting food for your family, to manifesting a promotion at work. It is what makes the world go around. It is ever evolving and mutating and weaving in and around your lives constantly and giving you reason to leave one moment for the next. With Hope of course. Accessing Hope in order to attain Manifestation is advisable. Hope is Knowing that Manifestation will occur and in time too. Hope is the lack of doubt and in so doing you welcome Manifestation into your lives so that you may create eagerly for your future. Manifestation is your true process working with God and spirit. Letting go of your human constraints of perception and expectation. For to Manifest you have to let go of expectations. Hope is better than expectations because it implies Knowing it will come about if it is meant to be. Expectations imply that it needs to happen or there will be failure and hence bad associating feelings. Expectations have origins in fear of lack. It shows that one is ever vigilant and ever watchful for results and taking your eyes off the goal or the job at hand. God and spirit, of course, don't want you to be disheartened yet encourage you to stay in Hope and Joy and Knowing in order to feel what it is you want coming to you. Having an open outlook actually lifts your vibration and increases your magnetism. You then start attracting to you progress and events that symbolise progress. You becoming aware of this ability is your lesson in this life. To start to work with spirit as opposed to wilfully on you own.

Of course, dear Loved One, We in no way mean you are wilful. However the act of not listening or heeding spirit is an act of wilfulness. This is fine because it shows your intention to grow and learn. However, not heeding intuition may lead you astray and you blame spirit for not guiding you away from problematic situations. We are strong enough to take it however We wait patiently for you to 'get' it and own your little mistakes. All is as it's meant to be and you will pass on to your children. Passing on this legacy ensures that they too will learn manifestation. Through seeing your Hope and your Joy and your Knowing. They will too have Hope, Joy and eventually Knowing. Giving your children this gift will ensure them their true survival. When We talk about survival We mean spiritually. We in no way mean that none of you will survive spiritually, what We mean is that your children will be self-sufficient in their understanding of how to manifest and in their love of God. Not to mention their trust in Him. We know that you love your children and that you will pass on what you know well. We want you to stay in the light of god in order maintain purity of guidance. With purity of guidance you can be assured that you will hit home with accuracy with regards to your aims and goals. This can only be of benefit to all those near to you such as your children.

Stay focussed on Manifestation and drawing to you what is in your highest interest. For this is working with the highest energy which will only ever bring about good. We don't wish for you to be despondent if Manifestation is not immediate. All is as it should be in that moment. You will ride it out and see for yourselves that with patience you will eventually see Manifestation for yourselves. God blesses you with Manifestation and gives it willingly and happily. See it like a secret bank account with valuables within it that you have never known existed and suddenly you realise all the wealth you've ever needed was there all along and all you had to do was ask and reach for it for yourself. Manifestation is truly your right. It is a tool designed specifically for you in order for you to learn to reach for life and reach for God. Manifestation is the promise of what time is yet to bring.

Existence

Existence just IS. You just simply, exist. We Angels just simply exist also. Existence lives throughout time and is the currency on which time rides. You simply exist and no amount of time can rob you of that. Time appears finite, yet it is not. It stretches out in all directions. Without Existence Time cannot be. Existence gives tangibility to Time. To be aware that you just exist means that Time flows through you and around you freely and you have not trapped it in order to control it. Time and Existence are interwoven and mutual. Would Time still be if Existence were not so? In some ways yes. However in order for it to be perceived Existence is needed. God has brought you into Existence because He wanted to experience life through you and to express Himself beautifully through you. This includes experiencing the seemingly passing of time through you. Time and waiting are intrinsically a part of your lives and you measure your Existence this way. Existence means that you are important. For you to exist you are undoubtedly integral to mankind. Each soul is important to the next. If one person was gone, missing, non-existent it ripples out over all of mankind. You are no less important than your politicians and heads of state. For without you your politicians would not be where they are now. All smaller organisms affect larger organisms. Forgive the analogy, We merely want to illustrate how each one of you is vital in the Existence of the greater organism. You are living, breathing aspects of, and expressions of God. Your Existence is hallowed and respected. Not a life is wasted nor ignored. All Existence is celebrated. For your time on Earth is precious and vital.

Your music demonstrates Time and its Existence. Music is a measurement of how sound flows through time. As the music is played you let go of awareness of time and let the music flow over you and through you letting go of all time constraints. In that moment of you listening to the music you forget time and Exist in the now. In this moment of releasement you go with time. You stop putting the pause button on time to assess where it is at in relation to your life. You let go and allow it to flow around you like water in a stream flowing around a stepping stone. Each stepping stone is important in order to get to the other side. Music is an exact measurement of rhythm and melody. You know that sometimes there is a 4/4 beat and words and melody are interwoven in, around and through it demonstrating creativity and intuitiveness even within certain structure. Despite the variances no one can argue that all works together and all are in Existence at the same time and each brings different perspectives and intentions to the table.

God has created your Existence in hopes that you will Love as only He knows how to Love. This is because you are a child of God and only He works through you. It is akin to owning a Gucci handbag. There is no doubting the pedigree of it and the quality cannot be denied. Having god work through you has no imitators and those that try fail miserably. Again dear Lisa We hear you laugh. Dear dear, We certainly must amuse. Do not forget God is ever present and omnipotent. You come from God and so your souls are timeless. Being human and mortal your body is the only finite part of you. So you see, dear Loved One, your Existence is timeless because you are a soul incarnating a body. Once your flesh and blood body ceases to exist you continue on to live in other bodies. Your Existence is continuous and everlasting and truly blessed. God loves you all equally and just as passionately. Existence means experiencing life and love. Love is running through everything and to have this Existence is yet another way to experience Love.

God truly values your Existence and the experiences all that you do in this Existence. He does not miss a thing that you do and celebrates with you and comforts you when you need support. Living in the moment, in the present you are in Existence. To live in the past is to live on the outskirts of Existence. Existence can only happen in the presence. We, dear Loved One, encourage you to endeavour to live in the present as you get much more out of your Existence that way. Isn't this exciting? That you know that you Exist and that you are powerful within this Existence. Power is not about dominance, it is about claiming your birthright and not allowing doubt to creep in. Doubt is a total drain on your Existence. Don't get Us wrong, dear Loved One, doubt is quite natural and is designed to magnify that which you should not do but most importantly what you SHOULD do. What you 'should' do is live life very present and aware of now and to trust in the process. Letting go of control.

Trusting God and spirit relieves you of burden. We Angels are realistic. We know that some of your experiences are significant and sometimes very traumatising. Yet We endorse that you still work with Us and God towards a positive outcome. Do you hear Us whisper to you? Those moments of clarity and motivation is usually a connection with Us that you cannot ignore. Please take heed as We have your best interests at heart and Love you unconditionally and are in service to God and mankind. God is ever present and loving. Do not feel you have strayed too far from home dear Loved One. For where ever you are We are and God is. Your wandering is but a perception. Come home to Us dear Loved One and see how magical it is to have a spiritual Existence. Blessed be you to Us Blessed be for now.

Afterword

I do hope you enjoyed this book and the previous two books in this trilogy. I don't see myself as writing these books as they kind of write themselves and obviously Arch Angel Gabriel was the driving force behind this communication. I was only the conduit. It may also be good to know that this book has been a healing for myself also as I wrote it. A lot happened synchronistically around me in order to guide me to the topics that the Angels wanted to talk about. I never knew one moment to the next what new topic would present itself. So this was a totally freestyle, intuitive and unplanned process. I was purely in Arch Angel Gabriel's capable hands and trusted Him totally that He knew what was best in writing this book.

I have had the other two books sitting there waiting for the third one to be written for nearly five years and this period in time must have been integral to writing this book in order to convey the right impression. I have a very busy life as a psychic medium, student, teacher and mum so finding the time and the energy was illusive. I finally had a break in my study and have been writing a page or two a day in between other aspects of my daily routine. A lot has happened in my life that has led me to believe that this is my true vocation. Writing books and spiritual practices. Even in my pastime of belly-dancing. More recently I have also taken to channelling Arch angel Gabriel to a small audience. I have developed a small close knit circle of people who attend and participate in a spiritual chat circle. I have my own unique brand of channelling and it seems to be beneficial to those who attend. This is by no means a method for me to find fame as I am shy of fame and glory. I want to stay humble and solution focussed.

To me, doing psychic readings was to help and motivate, not to be a main source of income. I never saw spirituality as business but as a service. I still struggle with t as it is now my job. However I find that many people actually need our services even if others are cynical of it. Working with Arch Angel Gabriel has been inspiring and cathartic for me. I am just as you, a consumer of spiritual books and a follower of spiritual leaders such as Doreen Virtue for they have led the way in making this way of being more mainstream and accessible. This book was dragged out of me because of my shyness and concern of losing my connection due to ego issues. Yet I have found that it has been easier than I thought and very helpful for me as well, I hope, as you.

I would sit for hours with my little Jack Russell/red heeler cross sitting at my feet. Or late at night with the cats all piled up on me to keep warm. It's not easy to type on a laptop with three purring furbodies on top of you. Originally I wrote the first two books in two weeks for each. My son was 12 nearly 13 and now he is 17 and a half and is six foot. He is my inspiration and has been the kick start in this industry for me. If it wasn't for him I would not be here talking to you. He, as a very small child, would see spirit and would regularly tell me of the old man who lived in his bedroom. We had the room cleansed and he had no more trouble. I would read books to understand this and found my own spirituality developing. I never in a million years expected to be writing books because I never saw myself as an intellectual. I was a doer. I was out there living life and not locked up in a room pondering life from a sage point. Yet as I was pushed, and I mean pushed, to write my first book I realised that life I had been living was what fuelled my point of reference and that I didn't have to lock myself away to write it. I would write in quiet moments when my son was at school or at scouts.

So here I am five years later a professional psychic medium and teacher and writing a book for Arch Angel Gabriel in order for Him to reach you. I sense Gabriel as male although many would say He is a She. However Angels are androgynous and no sex defined. Gabriel presents to me as male and I am ok with that. He is beautiful Angel and has a great sense of humour. He is around me constantly and provides me with the right thing to say. I am often forced to rewrite passages or even texts in order to convey what I want to say in the most effective way and I know it's to do with Gabriel. So I have learnt to listen to Him carefully in order to communicate well and with consideration for the other parties. I encourage you to connect with your Angels and in particular the Arch Angels.

Reading books like this are meditative and contemplative. It brings you into a space which is holy and peaceful. Until the next time, look after yourselves and make the world a better place.

Love and light. Lisa

Printed in Poland
by Amazon Fulfillment
Poland Sp. z o.o., Wrocław